From Menarche to Menopause

SUNY Series in Medical Anthropology
Setha M. Low, editor

From Menarche to Menopause

Reproductive Lives
of Peasant Women
in Two Cultures

YEWOUBDAR BEYENE

State University of New York Press

Published by
State University of New York Press, Albany

Printed in the United States of America

For information, address State University of New York
Press, State University Plaza, Albany, N.Y., 12246

Library of Congress Cataloging-in-Publication Data

Beyene, Yewoubdar.
    From menarche to menopause: reproductive lives of peasant women
  in two cultures/Yewoubdar Beyene.
        p.   cm.—(SUNY series in medical anthropology)
      Bibliography: p.
      Includes index.
      ISBN 0-88706-866-9. ISBN 0-88706-867-7 (pbk.)
      1. Menopause—Cross-cultural studies. 2. Menarche-Cross-cultural
    studies. 3. Mayas—Women. 4. Women, Greek. 5. Sex role—Cross-
    cultural studies. 6. Nature and nurture. I. Title. II. Series.
      [DNLM: 1. Cross-Cultural Comparison. 2 Menarche. 3. Menopause.
    WP 580 B573f]
    GN484.38.B48 1988
    305.4'2—dc19
    DNLM/DLC
    for Library of Congress   88-2244
               .   CIP

10 9 8 7 6 5 4 3 2 1

For my father, Beyene Reda, and my uncle, Hailu Araaya.
This accomplishment is the result of the values and
inspiration you instilled in me.

Contents

Figures   ix

Tables   xi

Acknowledgments   xiii

Funding Sources   xvii

1. Introduction   1

2. Current Assumptions about Menopause   11

3. Chichimila: A Mayan Village   27

4. Stira: A Mountain Village in Greece   49

5. Getting to Know the Women   67

6. Being a Woman in Chichimila   73

7. Being a Woman in Stira   89

8. Comparing Reproductive Histories, Part I: 103
      From Menarche through Childbearing

9. Comparing Reproductive Histories, Part II: 115
      Menopause in Two Cultures

10. Menopause: A Biocultural Event   127

Appendix: A Comparison of the Distribution of Fertility
      Patterns for Mayan and Greek Women   141

Bibliography   145

Index   163

Figures

Figures

1. Map of Chichimila   28

2. Map of Stira   50

3. Four Generations of Mayan Women   74

4. A Mayan Woman Weaving a Henequen Bag   75

5. Two Young Mayans Dancing "Jarana," Mayan Folk Dance   76

6. A Mayan Baby Girl   77

7. The Anthropologist with Two of Her Mayan
   Friends in Chichimila   78

8. Mayan Women Waiting to Vote for the 1981 Village Mayor   79

9. Three Generations of Greek Women   90

10. A Greek Woman Returning from Milking Her Goats   91

11. A Greek Woman Spinning Wool   92

12. A Greek Woman Crocheting for Her
    Granddaughter's Dowry   93

13. A Greek Woman Taking Hay to Her Livestock   94

14. The Village "Agora" (Center)   95

Tables

Tables

1. Characteristics of the Women of Chichimila, Yucatan   8

2. Characteristics of the Women of Stira, Evia   9

3. Comparison of the Distribution of Age at Onset   107
of Menarche for Mayan and Greek Women

4. Comparison of the Distribution of Menstrual Stages   129
of Mayan and Greek Women

5. Comparison of the Distribution of Age at Onset   130
of Menopause for Mayan and Greek Women

6. Comparison of the Distribution of Menopausal   131
Symptoms for Mayan and Greek Women

A. Marital Status of Women in Chichimila   141

B. Marital Status of Women in Stira   141

C. Comparison of Age at Birth of First Child   142

D. Comparison of the Distribution of Pregnancies for   142
Mayan and Greek Women

E. Comparison of Distribution of Number of Living   143
Offspring for Mayan and Greek Women

F. Comparison of Distribution of Child Mortality   143
for Mayan and Greek Women

Acknowledgments

From 1978 to 1979, as part of my academic training in medical anthropology, I worked as a program evaluator at the Northeast Community Mental Health Center in Cleveland, Ohio. My work consisted of in-take, counseling, case management and evaluation of the after care program for out-patients transferred from State Hospitals in Cleveland. A large number of these transferred patients were middle aged adults who had been under psychiatric care for several years. As part of the regular in-take interviews I asked each patient to tell me any events or circumstances that he or she felt were the direct or indirect causes for his or her illness. For the first six months of my work most patients' answers to this question were such events as anger, family fights, death of loved ones, unemployment, alcoholism and so forth. By then, doing in-take was routine and the answers to my specific questions were very familiar. However, one morning, a 60 year old woman who had been diagnosed with depression, introduced me to a new concept.

As the last item on the in-take form, I asked this woman to tell me what she thought was a cause for her condition. The woman looked around checking if there was any one except the two of us in the room and said in a very low voice, "you know, I never had this problem until I reached menopause." I said to myself, "menopause, I never knew menopause can cause depression." I asked the woman why she thought it was menopause that caused her depression. She said, "I don't know, dear. It was the doctor who told me that it is menopause that is making me feel depressed."

As my in-take interviews proceeded with the rest of the patient population, a few more middle aged women claimed that menopause was a major cause for their depression. After a while, I found the whole phenomenon of the causal relationship of menopause and depression very intriguing. Coming from a non-Western cultural background, I was not aware that menopause causes depression or any other emotional or physical illness. I only knew that menopause was a time when women in my culture felt free from the menstrual taboos; otherwise, no one pays any attention to this life event.

In order to satisfy my curiosity, I went to the library to search for information on the medical presentation as well as the sociocultural significance of menopause. The discrepancy that I found between the vast medical literature and the scanty anthropological information on this life event intensified my interest and led me to undertake the study of menopause for a dissertation topic.

For introducing me to a different concept of menopause, one that I was totally ignorant about, I would like to express my indeptedness to the anonymous women that I interviewed at Northeast Community Mental Health Center in Cleveland, Ohio.

Many people have contributed to the successful completion of this book in a variety of ways.

First, I would like to express my indebtedness to Professor Marie Haug for believing so strongly in this study and for sharing my enthusiasm for it from the beginning. She is responsible for the metamorphosis of this study from a class project to a dissertation and then to a book. As a principal investigator on the grant proposal that made funding possible for this project, she came for a site visit in Greece and debriefed me on my initial research findings. I am grateful to professor Haug for her continuous encouragement, constructive advice and indispensable editorial help throughout the early drafts of this project. I also would like to thank Dr. J. Kevin Eckert, a co-principal investigator on the grant proposal for this project and one of my dissertation committee members, for his help in designing the methodology for the study. He also came to Yucatan for a site visit to debrief me on my initial findings there. I thank Dr. Eckert for the hours he spent on this project.

Part of this book is a revised and edited version of my doctoral dissertation. I would like to express special thanks to Professor Allan Young, my academic advisor and my dissertation chairperson, for his constant support throughout my graduate education as well as for his time and effort as a dissertation chairperson. I also would like to thank Dr. Atwood

Gaines for is time and effort as one of my dissertation committee members.

Several people and institutions provided help during fieldwork. The final editing of the manuscript was completed during my tenure as Post-doctoral Research Fellow under a National Research Service Award of the National Institute on Aging, in the Medical Anthropology Program at the University of California, San Francisco. I would like to acknowledge the faculty and staff of the Medical Anthropology Program at the University of California for their support and invaluable feedback on this project. I also would like to acknowledge Dr. Sadja Greenwood in the Department of Obstetrics and Gynecology, University of California, San Francisco, for her comments on the last chapter of this book.

I am extremely grateful to Central College, Pella, Iowa, for allow-ing me to use their facilities in Yucatan. I would like to thank my very good friend, the Central College Program Director, Professor George Ann Huck, the Central faculty and staff who were in Yucatan at the time, for being kind to me.

Many thanks to my Mexican friends, Luis Ramirez, Silvia Teran and those in the Instituto Nacional Indiginista in Valladolid, for their interest in my work and for sharing their experiences with me.

Further acknowledgment goes to my Greek friends, Dr. Litsa Nicolaou-Smokovitis, our contact person in Greece, for her role in secur-ing local support, and to Dr. Periklis Aggeli, the rural doctor in Stira at the time, Maria Aggeli, Nicolaou and Elleni Levedis for their sup-port during fieldwork in Stira.

I would like to thank the people who must take immeasurable credit for helping me attain this goal. To Patterson and Elizabeth French, and Donald and Maxine Huffman, who gave me a home, love and support ever since I came to the United States. Without their initial help this goal would not have been started.

To all my Ethiopian friends and American colleagues who shared my ups and downs throughout this project, thank you for listening and caring.

The most important acknowledgment is due to the Mayan and Greek women who took me into their homes and shared their personal lives with me, without whom this study would have been impossible. Thank you for giving me the most memorable years of my life.

Funding Sources

The dissertation field research conducted entirely by the author, Yewoubdar Beyene, was supported in part by the National Institute on Aging, NIH, Grant No. RO1 AGO2622, *Menopause in Two Cultures—A Topical Ethnography,* for which Professor Marie R. Haug was listed as a principal investigator with Drs. J. Kevin Eckert and Yewoubdar Beyene as co-investigators. The author gratefully acknowledges this research support as well as Professor Haug's mentorship and legal release of Dr. Beyene's complete field data upon which this volume is based. Final preparation of the manuscript was supported by National Institute on Aging, NIH, under a National Research Service Award, Grant No. 5 T32 AG00045, *Training in Sociocultural Gerontology,* for which Professor M. Margaret Clark was the principal investigator. The author deeply acknowledges this support.

1

Introduction

Menopause is a universal female experience, but ways of reacting to it and interpreting it vary. In Western industrialized societies, this biological transition is assumed to have inevitable physiological and behavioral effects. Hormonal changes at menopause coincide with certain situational changes that seem to require social readjustments and medical treatment. In a youth-oriented culture such as in the United States, a woman must confront the unpleasant fact that she is aging. In the United States and in other industrialized Western societies, the disease model of menopause as a phenomenon is broadly accepted. In Western biomedical literature, menopause is defined as an estrogen deficiency disease or as an ovarian dysfunction producing a variety of somatic and/or behavioral complaints (Greenblatt and Bruneteau 1974, Utian 1980, Konichex 1984). Menopause is indexed in the *International Classification of Diseases* (1977).

In non-Western, nonindustrialized societies, as the reproducive role ceases, women may take on new social roles; in a culture where fertility is highly valued, menopause may have social and psychological ramifications. Although the ethnographic evidence is scanty, available research and experience thus far suggests that non-Western, nonindustrialized women often *do not* have the same psychological or phsyiological reactions to menopause as Western, industrialized women do. There is even a possibility that variations may exist in such basic physiological reactions as the tendency to osteoporosis, assumed by Western biomedicine as an inevitable concomitant of menopause.

1

Most frequently, explanations about changes in social role have been used to cover the lack of similar psychological and physiological symptoms between the two populations. In some cases, the fact that non-Western, nonindustrialized cultures do not have a disease model for menopause has been seen as a factor in what appears to be more positive experiences with menopause for women in those cultures.

However, little or no work has been done to cover the lack of physiological symptoms some nonindustrialized women show from a biocultural point of view. In addition, presumed psychological factors have been used to explain physiological evidence. While psychological responses are certainly profound and have definite physical effects, a systematic and holistic approach to the subject of menopause cannot leave out the effects of such environmental factors as diet or the physiologial impact of radically differing procreation patterns on the hormonal system. Moreover, the assumption that the new roles assumed by women in more traditional societies are completely positive, thereby accounting for a level of well-being sufficient to remove stress, has not been adequately tested. Finally, the connection between chronological age, role change, and menopause has not been extensively studied from a sociocultural point of view.

The relationship between the biophysical and behavioral factors of menopause has also been obscured by the tendency of Western biomedicine to conceive and define menopause as a disease episode rather than as a natural process. Some researchers question the universality of any of the consequences claimed for menopause by Western biomedicine.

One way to examine menopause, in order to differentiate the sociocultural from the physiological, is a cross-cultural comparison, enabling us to learn how this biological event is manifested in non-Western, nonindustrialized societies. However, most of the literature on menopause has been so far based on a Western biomedical model. Ethnographic reports covering menopause and findings related to the phenomenon are very scanty, anecdotal, inconsistent, or peripheral to other major topics of study (Murdock, 1963). Menopause as a topic of interest in anthropology is a recent phenomenon. Therefore, we have very little knowledge about the menopausal transition of women in non-Western, nonindustrialized societies with which to compare the menopausal transition of women in Western industrialized societies.

A few recent cross-cultural findings suggest that menopausal symptomatology may be culturally conditioned rather than physiologically induced (Bart, 1971; Datan, 1971; Flint, 1975; Griffin, 1977; 1982). These authors claim that variables such as removal of cultural taboos, positive role changes, and status gain at middle age have major effects on positive menopausal experiences in nonindustrialized societies.

The assumption that role stability and status gain have an effect on menopausal experience has, however, been challenged by Davis (1982). A woman's role and status changes in nonindustrialized societies do not necessarily correlate with nor depend on her menopausal age. Cross-cultural variation in menopausal experiences of women calls for explanation beyond social and cultural factors alone. Furthermore, the meaning and significance of menopause should be understood within the context of cultural interpretation of all reproductive phenomena unique to women, particularly menstruation, pregnancy, and the importance of fecundity. This study undertakes such a broad examination.

The data presented in this book were obtained from an extended ethnographic study that investigated and compared the natural history of reproductive experiences of women in cultures significantly unlike those of Western, industrialized societies. This book addresses the interrelated biocultural factors affecting menstruation, pregnancy, fecundity, and the social and physiological experiences of menopause. The cultures studied were rural Mayan Indians in Yucatan, Mexico, and rural Greek women living on the island of Evia, Greece. Selection of the cultures studied was based on two criteria: differences from dominant Western, industrialized cultural values concerning women and aging, and accessibility as a result of prior contact by the author.

In Greek peasant culture, the expressive roles of the woman within the family stress the quality of motherhood, not sexuality. The status of a woman increases with age (Campbell, 1964; Friedl, 1962). The life cycle of the traditional Greek woman is divided into three stages. The first is the unmarried girl, the "maiden." At this stage, a woman is secluded from the outside world; her clothes hide her femininity, and her hair is hidden under a scarf. She is viewed as cunning, and her cunning involves the corruption of men; she is considered a constant threat. The second stage is the married woman and mother. At this stage, the woman is no longer secluded. She is allowed to move about more freely and with less supervision, yet is still considered to be a sexual threat. Also, in the Greek tradition, a menstruating woman is considered impure. She is prohibited from participating in religious activities for fear of the damage that could result from her impurity (du Boulay, 1974; Blum and Blum, 1965.)

The final stage of a woman's life is the period between the marriage of her eldest son and her death. At this time, the woman gains a new freedom from the authority of her husband and the restrictions of social convention. As a mother of honorably married sons and daughters, she transcends the earlier beliefs pertaining to the inferiority of women and takes on new and more powerful roles. For example, she becomes pivotal within the extended family and a focus of her sons' cooperation. She is a model to her daughters-in-law, and a midwife who delivers their children and provides them with support and encouragement. During the sixth decade of life, the sexuality of women is no longer an important consideration. Women at this stage are considered to have clean souls (Campbell, 1964; Blum and Blum, 1965).

In the Mayan society, age is associated with increased power and respect. Every young person is responsible to and respectful toward three pairs of older persons: biological parents, godparents and parents-in-law (Redfield, 1934; Whitlock, 1976). Respect for elders within the family, especially toward the mother is very pronounced (Steggerda, 1941). The older woman in Mayan culture is the head of the family. She has responsibility for allocating the family's resources. She may also function as midwife and healer (Elmendorf, 1976; Redfield, 1934). While younger women are not allowed to participate in religious activities, older women are given an opportunity to take part in some religious festivals (de Landa, 1978).

In this culture, a large part of the concept of time and age is on an annual basis, tied to the planting of corn, the ripening of fruit, the annual fiestas, and even the days of the births and deaths of family members and friends. People are less likely to remember the year of an event than the day and the month it occurred. The exact times and ages of things are of minor importance to them. Years are lived, not added (Elmendorf, 1976).

The Greek and Mayan populations studied clearly show reactions to and interpretations of menopause that differ from the usual Western biomedical model. This study seeks to provide an ethnography of menopause within the context of the reproductive history of women in nonindustrialized communities, using the Greek and Mayan women as examples. The central aim of ethnography is to understand another way of life from the native point of view. Rather than "studying people," *ethnography* means "learning from people." Thus, the essential core of ethnography is a concern with what actions and events mean to the people. Some of these meanings are directly expressed in language while others are indirectly communicated through actions and behavior (Spradley, 1979). People learn their culture by making inferences. In order to make cultural.inferences one observes what people do, what they make and use, and what they say (Spradley, 1980).

The overall research design comprised two stages conducted over twelve months at each research site, Chichimila and Stira. Participant observation was a very important part of the research methodology, enabling me to win the confidence of the villagers. Because the topics of menstruation and menopause are very personal issues and are not freely discussed with any stranger, it was necessary to spend a good part of the research time building friendships with the women in the communities. This was done by participating in the daily activities of women. This, in turn, gave me the opportunity to engage in general conversation with the women on different topics, including menstruation, menopause, the status of older women, attitude toward aging, and other related areas. This situation also allowed the women to get to know me and to ask any questions they had, personal as well as cultural. This type of relationship was important in order to get an overview of the meaning and definitions of *menopause* and to make detailed behavioral observations of activities that these women engage in at home and in other settings. Direct participation in the everyday life of the women also allowed me to observe the individual woman in the context of her household and family.

This book attempts to provide a holistic view of peasant women and the cultural significance and physiological manifestation of menopause in two nonindustrialized cultures. A *holistic approach* means studying a culture totally: the economic, religious, political, and social dimensions of a particular culture as it affects its people. Cross-cultural studies of menopause should consider the social and economic status of the women as well as their personal lives, reproductive histories, health beliefs, and practices in order to present a complete picture of these women. Comparison of menopausal experiences of one group of peasant women to another group makes isolating historical, cultural, and environmental factors relating to variations or similarities in response to menopause possible.

Methods of Data Gathering

In each culture, the first stage of the research employed intensive participant observation of women in their natural settings, census taking and mapping, and informal, unstructured interviews with key informants.

Census Taking and Mapping

According to the census taken by the Mexican government office in June 1981, Chichimila had a population of 2,300. Data from the village registrar indicated that Stira had a population of 450 in September of 1982. Once the sites for the research were selected, I mapped out the spatial relationships of significant physical features of the communities. I also took my own census of the village households with the help of native teenage girls in each culture. The census included data on the heads of households, the number of persons living in each family, age, sex, education, and occupation. Census was also done in the adjacent village, Kapsala, because it was clear at the beginning that Stira alone would not secure a large enough number of Greek women for the study. The formal sample of women is based on this census.

Informal and Unstructured Interviews

During this initial phase of participant observation, I obtained data on women and their roles and activities, conducting unstructured and informal interviews with persons in the communities. Unstructured interviews were conducted with key informants such as older women, traditional healers, midwives, and medical personnel in the health services and clinics that served the villagers. As the process of participant observation and informal interviewing unfolded, a series of culturally relevant categories of information was developed around the issues of the menopausal experiences of women in the villages, which became the topics for the formal interviews.

Life History Interviews

Once preliminary analysis of the fieldnotes and records from Stage I was completed, structured life history interviews with approximately 105 Mayan women and 96 Greek women began.

These interviews focused on the life histories of the subjects and topics of special interest that emerged during Stage I. Along with the experience of and attitudes toward menopause, topics included the history of pregnancy, health, experience of and attitudes toward menstruation, aging, and dietary habits. Each interview was conducted in the language spoken by the women and the interviews were tape recorded and transcribed. The languages used were Greek and Spanish, and all interviews were conducted by me. Consent was obtained from all respondents to tape-record the interviews. The tapes were erased after the accuracy of the transcriptions had been verified.

Selection of respondents for the life history interviews was based on the census data gathered earlier, which provided a list of every household with adult women. Of the availabe adult women, those who were 40 years old and older were selected as potential interview candidates. Approximately 35 women were selected from three age cohorts, corresponding to what are, according to biomedical notions, the three stages of menopause: those 40 to 49 years were expected to be "premenopausal," 50 to 55 years, "menopausal" and older than 55 years, "postmenopausal." The specific age cohorts represented a preliminary estimate of menstrual stage groups. Women who were still menstruating were defined as *premenopausal;* those who had not been menstruating for six months prior to the interview and those with irregular menses (provided that menstruation had previously been regular) were defined as *menopausal.* Women who had completely ceased menstruating for one year or more were defined as *postmenopausal.*

Demographic Characteristics of Subjects in Chichimila and Stira

Women from the different age categories were selected for detailed life history interviews. The size of the general population did not allow for random sampling. Thus, all women in the appropriate age category for the study were selected from the census taken during Stage I and were approached for interviews. Before the questionnaires were administered, they were pretested on pre- and postmenopausal women in the villages who were not in the study sample and all necessary adjustments were made. Throughout the research in both cultures, I was assisted by a native woman, respected and well-known by the rest. The assistant in each village introduced me to the various households from which I collected the data. The assistant in Chichimila also helped interpret from Maya to Spanish whenever I interviewed a woman who could not speak Spanish. Consent was obtained from all respondents to tape-record the interviews and after each interview was over the individual was allowed to hear her recorded voice. All names in the text are pseudonyms.

In Chichimila, 107 women were interviewed for the study; 36 of the women were in the premenopausal group, 36 in the menopausal group, and 35 in the postmenopausal (see Table 4). The actual ages of the women ranged from 33 to 57 years old. My initial assumption was that women in between the ages of 40 and 55 would represent the different menstrual stage groups. However, as interviews proceeded, the distribution across the categories appeared markedly unequal among the women, because the onset of menopause proved to occur earlier than it generally does in the United States and other industrialized countries. Thus, the age criterion had to be adjusted downward to provide approximately equal numbers of subjects at each menstrual stage.

Of the 107 women, 93 were married, one divorced, three separated, four widowed, five were single, and one cohabiting. For those who were married, the mean age at first marriage was 18.5 years. With regard to their husbands' occupations, 70 were farmers, four merchants, four venders, two bricklayers, two carpenters, ten worked in Can Cun, and eight did not have specific jobs. The mean number of pregnancies for those who had children was seven, with 4.7 of the children surviving the first year of life (see Table 1).

Table 1
Characteristics of the Women of Chichimila, Yucatan (N=107)

	Average Age	SD	Range
Current age	42.5	5.7	33–57
Age at menarche	13.3	1.5	11–17
Age at marriage	18.6	4.5	13–40
Age at birth of first child	20.0	4.0	14–35
Age at menopause	42.0	4.4	33–55
Number of pregnancies	7.0	3.7	0–17
Number of miscarriages	1.3	1.5	0–6
Number of children died	1.1	1.4	0–6
Number of living children	4.7	2.7	0–11
Husband's age	48.1	8.5	31–77

In Stira, of the 96 women interviewed for the study, 30 were premenopausal, 31 menopausal, and 35 postmenopausal (see Table 4). The actual ages of the women range from 38 to 59 years old. Of the 96 women, 92 were married, three were widowed, and one never married. For those who were married, the mean age of first marriage was 24.5 years. With regard to their husbands' occupations, 62 were farmers, four merchants, two carpenters, six quarrymen, two worked outside of the village, and eight did not have fixed jobs. The mean number of pregnancies for those who had children was 2.9, with 2.5 of the children surviving the first year of life (see Table 2).

Table 2
Characteristics of the Women of Stira, Evia (N=96)

	Average Age	SD	Range
Current age	48.7	5.4	38–59
Age at menarche	14.0	1.9	11–18
Age at marriage	24.4	5.0	14–39
Age at birth of first child	26.0	4.8	16–39
Age at menopause	47.0	5.0	32–54
Number of pregnancies	2.9	1.9	0–15
Number of miscarriages	0.6	1.1	0–6
Number of children died	0.08	0.3	0–1
Number of living children	2.5	1.2	0–8
Husband's age	55.0	7.3	40–73

Overview

The first chapter of this book outlines the issues and structure of the book. Chapter two provides an overview of the literature on menopause, addressing the physiological, psychological, social, and cultural factors related to menopause and recent trends in Western culture. Chapters three and four describe the research site in Yucatan: the village where the research was undertaken, the people and their lifesytles, economy, social organization, and health beliefs and practices, including the socialization of women and their roles and status in the Mayan culture. Chapters five and six describe the research site in Greece and the socialization of women and their roles and status in Greek peasant community. Chapter seven describes my adjustment and experiences as an anthropologist of Ethiopian extraction in being accepted in the two study sites. Chapter eight provides a reproductive history of women studied in both cultures; it compares menarche, the perception of menstruation, and the importance of fecundity and pregnancy in the Mayan and Greek peasant societies. Chapter nine provides an ethnographic description of menopause in the two cultures. The final chapter compares the menopausal experiences of Mayan and Greek women and discusses possible explanations that could account for the difference in menopausal experiences of women in these two different cultures, concluding that, as with other developmental events, menopause is a biocultural experience and proposes that research on menopause should consider biocultural factors such as environment, diet, and fertility patterns that may be involved in the variations of menopausal experience. Overall, the book provides not only new data on menopause, but also hypotheses for further investigations of menopause and new insights into the general study of women and aging, particularly with regard to the problem of osteoporosis. It documents the existence of alternative realities of menopause in their natural terms, thereby providing an ethnography of menopause.

2

Current Assumptions about Menopause

Indicative of the problems in making assumptions about menopause is the fact that the term *menopause* is sometimes used loosely. Although many people use *menopause* and *climacteric* interchangeably, referring to a woman's "change of life," the terms need to be distinguished from each other. The *climacteric* refers to a transition phase, occurring approximately between the ages of 45 and 60, which involves gradual changes in all body tissues for both men and women. *Menopause*, on the other hand, occurs during the climacteric phase and refers specifically to the cessation of menstruation, an end to a woman's reproductive capacity (Seaman and Seaman, 1977; Utian and Serr, 1976).

The human life cycle is punctuated by critical biological points. For the adolescent, the onset of puberty is such an event. For the mature woman, menopause represents a biologically determined critical point. Like puberty, it is known to entail profound endocrine and somatic changes and is often associated with identifiable psychological effects and social repercussions. In many societies, the hormonal changes at menopause coincide with certain changes in a woman's social situation. In the youth-oriented culture of the West, such as in the United States, menopause is a symbolic milestone on the way to old age. In cultures where a woman's social and personal identity is closely tied to her fertility, menopause marks the passage to a new social identity and changed concepts of self.

Although menopause is a universally occurring, natural biological phenomenon, in some societies women experience few, if any, of the physiological and psychological symptoms of which Western women commonly complain in connection with menopause (Dowty et al., 1970; Flint, 1975; Maoz et al., 1977). In spite of this, the Western medical system has tended to approach menopause in terms of a disease paradigm (Rothman, 1979). As previously noted, menopause is indexed in the *International Classification of Diseases* (1977). In Western biomedical literature menopause is defined as an estrogen deficiency disease or as an ovarian dysfunction producing a variety of somatic and/or behavioral complaints (Wilson, 1963; Greenblatt and Bruneteau, 1974; Utian, 1980; Koninchx, 1984). However, physicians differ in their opinions concerning appropriate medical intervention for menopausal complaints (Lennane and Lennane, 1973; Lock, 1982).

In fact, no consensus is found among physicians, social scientists, feminists, and the general population concerning the symptoms, both biological and behavioral, associated with menopause. When menopausal experiences of women in different Western cultures are compared, considerable variability is found in the incidence of most symptoms. The only symptoms systematically associated with the menopause are hot flashes (Greene and Cook, 1980; Kaufert and Syrotuik, 1981; McKinlay and Jefferys, 1974; Mikkelsen and Holte, 1982; Wood, 1979). While most Western physicians agree that hot flashes and cold sweats are the direct results of hormonal decline, considerable disagreement exists about psychosomatic and psychological symptoms of the menopausal syndrome. Nonspecific and amorphous symptoms such as headaches, dizziness, fatigue, anxiety, insomnia, depression, and general emotional problems associated with menopause are considered less likely to be directly related to such changes (Greene and Cook, 1980; Bungay et al., 1980; Wood, 1979).

A review of the standard literature on menopause and its impact on health shows gaps and conflicting findings. The following discussion of the mainstream Western literature is organized according to the physiological, psychological, feminist, social, and cultural assumptions under discussion.

Mainstream Western Ideas

Physiological Factors

In Western medical literature, menopause and climacteric are viewed as the consequences of aging of the ovaries, a gradual process that occurs during the period between menarche and menopause. The changes that occur in the ovaries influence the hypothalamic-pituitary unit and its hormone production and the functions of the ovary itself (Peters, 1978). Menopause is believed to occur when there are fewer primordial follicles (oocytes) in the ovary and the remaining follicles are unresponsive, showing no signs of development despite large amounts of circulating gonadotropins (follicle stimulating hormone and luteotrophic hormone). As a result, lower levels of circulating estrogen and progestrone are found because the follicles do not mature (Carroll, 1983).

Before menopause, the main source of estradiol is direct secretion by the ovaries. After menopause, the ovaries secrete insignificant quantities of estrogens (Thijssen and Longcope, 1976). This ovarian insufficiency results in estrogen deficiency with its attendant problems (Lauritzen, 1976; Utian, 1979; Wilson and Wilson, 1963; Greenblatt, 1974). Research based on the medical model indicates that vasomotor changes such as hot flashes and sweating, as well as atrophic vaginitis, become common when menstrual periods stop (Achte, 1970; Berr, 1975; Wentz, 1976). The typical hot flash consists of a sudden onset of feelings of warmth, usually occurring over the anterior chest, spreading to the neck and face, and associated with sweating and sometimes with chills. Vasomotor changes, such as hot flashes, have been attributed to both estrogen decrease and gonadotropin increase (Friederich, 1982; Voda, 1982; Bohler and Greenblatt, 1974). The estrogen deficiency syndrome also includes metabolic alterations. Indeed, some researchers have shown that the cessation of estrogen production is a major factor determining the occurrence of osteoporosis in women, a reduction in bone density per unit of bone volume and increasing disposition toward bone fracture. Thus, early menopause or early surgical oophorectomy without replacement therapy is often associated with lower bone mass at an earlier age and increased incidence of osteoporotic fractures (Nordin, 1982; Richelson et al., 1984; Lindsay, 1984; Lindsay et al., 1980, Genant et al., 1982). Although this is a normal aging phenomenon occuring in both men and women, the incidence of bone fracture seems to increase for menopausal women without any increase among men of the same age group (Friederich, 1982; Nordin, 1982).

The single most important factor associated with loss of bone is malabsorption of calcium. When estrogenic hormones become deficient, other hormones (such as parathyroid hormone, the function of which is to maintain the plasma calcium concentration) become relatively more potent and resorb bone more easily. This increased sensitivity of bone to parathyroid hormone produces loss of bone within one year of the manopause and continues at an average rate of 1 percent per annum until the end of life (Nordin, 1982).

Vasomotor instability and metabolic changes are caused by the decrease of estrogens below a threshold level and may be ameliorated or even removed altogether if these hormones are replaced. In addition to the vasomotor changes, some researchers consider that symptoms of depression, irritability, and emotional instability during menopause are due to hormonal changes, that is, estrogen deficiency snydrome (Koninchx, 1984; Utian, 1980; Notelovitz, 1978; Lauritzen, 1976; Cooper, 1976; Furuhjelm and Fedor Freybergh, 1976; Greenblatt, 1974; Wilson and Wilson, 1963). Research (Ballinger, 1976, 1977; Brown and Brown, 1976), indicates that other symptoms commonly associated with menopause, for example, headaches, dizziness, palpitation, sleeplessness, depression, and irritability, do not have clear temporal relations with it.

Psychological Factors

In the West, menopausal women are believed to suffer not only from functional and organic disorders, but also from widely differing psychological complaints, such as loss of concentration, fatigue, emotional instability, depression, irritability, frustration, a sense of inadequacy, and so on (Dennerstein and Burrows, 1978; Kopera, 1978). From the psychoanalytic point of view, menopausal symptoms are seen as a reaction to a loss of femininity. A woman experiences the cessation of the menstrual cycle as a lowering of her self-esteem: menopause is a time of disappointment and mortification. Hormonally induced changes in the body (for example, deepening of voice, weight gain) and decline in sexual attractiveness occur, and such biological change is experienced by some women as object loss.

Depression results when the object lost is invested with the loser's self-esteem (Engel, 1962). Deutsch (1945) referred to the loss of reproductive capacity as "a partial death." From the psychoanalytic perspective the central feature of the menopause is anxiety, and its most potent cause is the threat that menopause directs toward the ego. The threat operates principally at the instinctual level but also, to some extent, at the level of consciousness. Both by inherent impulse and by decades of conditioning, reproductive activity is a fundamental, symbolic token of female personal worth. Thus, menopause symbolizes the loss of this capacity and causes a woman to relive castration anxiety (Fessler, 1950; Hoskins, 1944). Women experiencing a lowering of self-esteem and loss of femininity may become increasingly prone to depression. Menopause is viewed as a time of loss and a time of mourning; therefore, women will probably experience some distress as they reevaluate their position (Brown, 1976; Achte, 1970; Hoskins, 1944). However, using a sample of 114 women aged 45 to 50, clinically identified as possible psychiatric cases, Ballinger (1976) found no evidence of any specific combination of symptoms and signs associated with the cessation of menstrual periods.

Social and Economic Factors

Western women's experience of menopausal symptoms may· also be influenced by other role transitions. During the menopausal years, women are faced with the reality of growing older, with declining physical attractiveness in a culture that stresses youth and youthful beauty to an extreme degree. Children have become teenagers or young adults and have left or are leaving home. This is the time when parents age and die, and husbands reach a plateau in their careers and may show an increasing investment of energy and interest away from home (Brown and Brown, 1976; Friederich, 1982; Parlee, 1976). These changes demand further readjustment beyond the fact of menopause per se. Feeling overwhelmed as a result of role change may cause anxiety and depression that can, in turn, interact with other menopausal problems. For example, a mother may find it difficult to redirect her life after her children have left home, particularly if she faces increased demands from her husband.

Women who have been full-time homemakers must turn to the community in order to find meaningful activities for living. If they have been in the work arena, they have frequently reached their employment potential and are actively engaged in careers. They may well be looking inward, questioning values, wondering if they wish to change their current life situations. They are aware of limited time ahead in which to accomplish what they wish to do. From the perspective of the woman, such role changes and adjustments may be of greater importance than the biological fact of cessation of menstruation. Indeed, some argue that life situation is more important than endocrine changes in producing psychiatric symptoms at this time of life (Achte, 1970; Ballinger, 1975; Brown and Brown, 1976; Friederich, 1982; Greene, 1983).

It is variously suggested that menopausal symptoms other than hot flashes are due to factors such as "empty nest" syndrome (Parlee, 1979), negative attitudes toward aging, role changes (Flint, 1975; Griffen, 1977), perceived loss of femininity (Deutsch, 1945; Fessler, 1950), and a generally negative attitude toward menopause and aging in Western cultures.

However, epidemiological studies indicate that the above mentioned factors do not necessarily make women susceptible to developing symptoms at the menopause. Nonspecific symptoms appear to be associated with preexisting psychological and economic difficulties (Holte and Mikkelsen, 1982; Uphold and Susman, 1981; Schneider and Brotherto, 1979; Severne, 1979).

Other studies suggest that social class (van Keep and Kellerhals, 1974), work roles, and socioeconomic status (Severne, 1979; Schneider, 1979; McKinlay and Jefferys, 1974) are important factors in mediating the response to menopause. Crawford and Hooper (1973), in their study of 106 middle-class and working-class women in England, concluded that little evidence is found to support the idea that menopause is a critical transition, unless it is associated with other life events.

Western Feminist Critique

In recent years the medical diagnosis and treatment of menopausal symptoms by the Western medical system has come under strong criticism, particularly by feminist authors and the National Women's Health Organization Movement in the United States, which represents women's health groups in the United States, both health professionals and consumers. The major focus of this organization is on education and health policy legislation to improve the quality of women's health care.

A growing body of literature on menopause written by feminist researchers (Reitz, 1977; Scully, 1980; Seaman and Seaman, 1977; Voda and Eliasson, 1983) indicates that a conscious attempt exists to create a new image in which the transitions and the last part of the life cycle are viewed as a time of growth rather than loss. These authors reaffirm that menstruation, childbirth, and menopause are natural events that, in most cases, do not need medical intervention.

Some (Griffin, 1983; McCrea, 1983; MacPherson, 1981) feel that the management of menopause by male physicians in the Western medical system reduces a complex psychological and cultural process to a physiological, and therefore medical-clinical, level. The National Women's Health Organization and other feminists challenge the legitimacy of the disease model of menopause. They argue that the menstrual and menopausal myths, by describing women's physical and mental capabilities as dependent on their reproductive cycles, are a form of social control, through which the health care system in Western culture legitimates sexism and ageism under the guise of science.

For example, the National Women's Health Organization Movement defined the health care system, including estrogen treatment, as a serious social problem. The male-dominated medical profession was accused of reflecting and perpetuating a social ideology that views women as sex objects and reproductive organs (MacPherson, 1981; Posner, 1979; McCrea, 1983). Authors, such as Ehrenreich and English in *Complaints and Disorder: The Sexual Politics of Sickness* (1973), analyzed medical beliefs and practices relating to women in the United States from 1865 to 1920. Their work traced the history of the medicalization of the female reproductive cycle in the United States and the redefinition and transformation of natural phenomena such as childbirth and menopause. During this period, according to Ehrenreich and English (1973), doctors defined pregnancy and menopause as disease, menstruation as a chronic disorder, and childbirth as a surgical event.

Science was invoked to justify the social inequities imposed along sexual lines, just as it had been used to legitimize domination based on race and class. Espousing the same position as Ehrenreich and English, MacPherson (1981) points out that the transformation of menopause into a disease has been a gradual and collective political achievement, rather than the inevitable outcome of the natural evolution of society or the progress of medical science. Thus, the historical development of female roles and sexuality in America helped create the passivity of women in the nineteenth and twentieth centuries, while male physicians transformed normal reproductive cycle experiences (menses, childbirth, and menopause) into diseases.

During the nineteenth century, Victorian physicians played a major role in creating the female biological imperative. They saw women as prisoners of their reproductive system; their uterus and ovaries controlled their bodies and behavior from puberty through menopause. On the other hand, the male reproductive system was assumed to exert no parallel degree of control over men's bodies or minds. With the advent of Freudian psychology in the early twentieth century, menopause was viewed as neurosis; and as synthetic estrogens become readily available in the 1960s, physicians treated menopause as a deficiency disease (McCrea, 1983; MacPherson, 1981). Freudian psychoanalysis has also helped keep women controlled and dominated by men by persuading women to believe that their problems are intrapsychic rather than social, economic, or political. Freud theorized that at menopause, the absence of menstruation is reexperienced by woman as the psychological loss she once felt in early childhood, when she compared her body to a boy's for the first time and concluded that she had been castrated. MacPherson (1981) states that physicians extended the boundaries of their roles beyond diagnosis and treatment of the usual diseases to include the definition and management of the normal female condition. Western medicine also extended its power as an agent of social control by stating that physicians should care for all women in menopause.

During the 1960s, Robert A. Wilson, a New York gynecologist, led the crusade to redefine menopause as a physical disease. In his book, *Feminine Forever* (1966), Wilson stated that in the course of his work, spanning four decades and involving hundreds of carefully documented clinical cases, it became evident that menopause is, in fact, a deficiency disease. To cure diabetes, he said, physicians supply the lacking substance in the form of insulin. A similar logic can be applied to menopause: the missing hormones can be replaced. As founder and head of the Wilson Foundation, established in 1963 to promote estrogen therapy and supported by $1.3 million in grants from the pharmaceutical industry, Wilson's writings were crucial to the large-scale, routine administration of estrogen replacement therapy (ERT) (McCrea, 1983; MacPherson, 1981).

Wilson's claim was supported by a number of prominent U. S. physicians. For example, one of his strong supporters, Robert Greenblatt (1974) claimed about 75 percent of menopausal women are acutely estrogen deficient and advocated ERT for them. Throughout the late 1960s and early 1970s, Wilson's book, *Feminine Forever,* (1966), was excerpted widely in traditional women's journals, and more than 300 articles promoting estrogen appeared in popular magazines. During the same period, an aggressive advertising campaign capitalizing on the disease label was launched by the U. S. pharmaceutical industry. ERT products were widely advertised in medical literature and promotional material as amelioratives for a variety of psychological as well as somatic problems (McCrea, 1983).

The National Women's Health Organization Movement has argued that menopause is not an event that in itself limits women's psychological or physical capacities, but a natural part of aging. They feel that the aging woman has a particularly vulnerable social status in Western society. She is no longer the object of adoration and romanticism that youthful women frequently are. Menopause usually comes at a time when children leave home, and husbands may seek younger sexual partners. Physical changes taking place in her body may be followed by loss of status and primary social role. Thus, the socially vulnerable status of women is fertile ground for medical imperialism. Moreover, a health care system based on fee-for-service is conducive to defining more and more life events as illnesses. Thus, a disease definition of *menopause* has served the interests of both the medical profession and the pharmaceutical industry.

The feminists argue that menstruation, childbirth, and menopause are natural events. Moreover, unlike the Western biomedical pronouncement of menopause as a crisis event or an illness state, several studies (Neugarten et al., 1963; McKinlay and Jefferies, 1974; Feely and Pyne, 1975; Frey, 1982; McKinlay and McKinlay, 1985; Leiblum and Swartzman, 1986; Kaufert and Gilbert, 1986) show that menopause is not seen by most Western women as a central or distressing event, and they do not find much difficulty going through this stage. McKinlay and McKinlay (1985) point out that physicians derive their statistically biased stereotypical image of Western menopausal women from a group of atypical women with surgical oophorectomy.

Overall, women tend to agree that menopausal symptoms such as hot flashes are brought about by changes in estrogen levels; however, regardless of the discomfort these symptoms bring, they do not view menopause as an illness (Frey, 1982). Furthermore, Western women are more apt to attribute psychological difficulties that occurred around the menopause to distressing life changes than hormonal fluctuations. Moreover, a study done by Leiblum and Swartzman (1986) indicates that female sexuality remains strong subsequent to menopause. Sexual interest and comfort increase following the menopause and 91 percent of the women surveyed disagree with the notion that male partners of menopausal women regard them as less sexually desirable following the menopause. They also disagree with the notion that a woman loses her femininity after menopause.

However, these studies (Frey, 1982; Leiblum and Swartzman, 1986; LaRocco and Polit, 1980) also indicate a strong relationship between attitude toward the menopause and occupational status. Women in professional occupations had the highest wellness orientation toward menopause and those least educated had the most illness-oriented responses and were more likely to subscribe to a medical model of menopause. These studies suggest that career orientation and type of occupation may have a significant influence on an individual's experience at the time of menopause.

In short, feminists argue that social and cultural factors have shaped women's expectations and behavior so that they experience unnecessary psychological and somatic changes at menopause. Therefore, they call for a dismantling of the present disease metaphor.

Cross-Cultural Assumptions

The few studies available suggest that response to menopause is conditioned by the cultural context that shapes the pattern of a woman's roles. Such studies view culture as an organized system that attributes meanings to reality, thereby giving each natural phenomenon a particular meaning and significance. Within a given society, the perceptions held by subcultural groups often vary from those of the dominant group. Thus, the meanings attached to pregnancy, menstruation, menopause, and disease vary within one culture as well as among cultures (van Keep and Kellerhals, 1974). The dominant view in Western culture associates the menopausal role with lowered status and emotional and physical distress.

For example, Neugarten (1968), in her study of American women's attitude toward menopause, indicated that in the United States, most young women have a negative view of menopause. This might be because menopause is a part of the entire process of growing old, a process that is considered unpleasant in a youth and production-oriented society. For example, women, including nurses, were asked to identify the first thing that came to mind when they heard the word "menopause." Their responses included loss of youth, depression, hot flashes, empty nest, fatigue, over-the-hill, and midlife crisis (Carroll, 1983). Moreover, the process of menopause is medically defined and treated as such (Dougherty, 1978; Rothman, 1979; Seaman and Seaman, 1977). A study of 1,708 Caucasian American and 1,221 Japanese American women in Hawaii (Goodman, Stewart, and Gilbert, 1977) suggested that the use of medical treatment is related to differences in menopausal experiences of women from the two cultural backgrounds. The frequency of surgery and medication for female disorders before and after menopause is greater for Caucasian women than for Japanese women.

Although no cross-cultural studies specifically concerned with women's response to menopause exist, some research has touched on the phenomenon peripherally. Many non-Western cultures, for example, Islamic societies and most African societies, clearly define the distinctions between male and female by taboos and social sanctions (Douglas, 1966). In these societies, postmenopausal women are no longer obligated to observe them. They may be unveiled, released from seclusion, and may participate in men's talking and drinking. They are no longer considered contaminating agents, a significant change from their menstruating and child-bearing years.

An example of the way such release from role constraints may be seen to affect the physiological experience of menopause is suggested by Flint (1975). In the course of her research, she found that among the Rahjput classes in Indian, where women are rewarded for having reached the end of the fertility period, very few have problems with menopause other than changes in menstruation. Flint found no depression, dizziness, or incapacitation due to menopause. Flint compared this with the severity of symptoms among women in North America. She suggests that the explanation for the difference in menopausal experiences between North American women and the Rahjput women may be that the latter are permitted significant positive role changes at menopause. Flint makes associations between menopausal symptoms and events such as empty nest syndrome and marriage crisis, that may or may not occur simultaneously with the menopause.

However, Davis (1982) has challenged the assumption that role stability and status gain have a positive effect on menopausal experiences. The data from her Newfoundland sample indicate that no link existed between positive attitude toward menopause and higher status. She found that status was important mainly as it related to the resources women drew upon to cope with menopause.

Maoz and colleagues (1977) in their study of Israeli women of five different subcultural groups found a somewhat similar situation. They found that women who were Arabs and North Africans suffered few or no menopausal symptoms: menopause was not a time of crisis for them, nor was it viewed negatively. On the other hand, menopause elicited either a mixed or negative attitude from the European sample.

In Wales, Skultans (1970) found that menopause was seen as a rite of passage, marking the transition from a reproductive to a nonreproductive role. In the course of her research in Wales, she observed that women did not have a negative attitude toward hot flashes. In fact, they believed it is necessary to experience hot flashes as frequently as possible during menopause, otherwise dangerous complications could develop. Hot flashes are thought to result from menstrual blood rushing to the head; the absence of flashes implies a deficiency of menstrual blood. Flashes are thought to carry women through the change more quickly and safely. Some menopausal women regretted that their flashes were not frequent enough. Skultans's writing is based on 18 informants and does not represent all menopausal Welsh women.

In a review of the ethnographic data in the Human Relations Area File (HRAF), Griffen (1977, 1982) compared behavioral changes at menopause cross-culturally. Behavioral changes range from total withdrawal from previous social activities to participation in previously prohibited roles. Griffen stated that existing cross-cultural data indicate that increased freedom of behavior is a very real possibility for postmenopausal women in some cultures. She also indicates that in some cultures women may be considered less useful or less valuable after their childbearing years. The apparent freedom of older women in various cultures contrasts with the modesty expected from women of childbearing potential (Griffen, 1982; Flint, 1975). Freedom from this constraint might indicate that elderly women are no longer viewed as appropriate sex objects (Ardener, 1977). Griffen (1977, 1982) concludes that the postmenopausal female is strongly shaped by her culture, as well as by the choices she makes as an individual. Griffen realizes that her conclusions based on the insufficient data from the HRAF are tentative. Her conclusions are based on 10 percent of the files containing material relevent to the climacteric.

Townsend and Carbone (1980), on the other hand, question whether such transitions, for example, participation in male activities, (mentioned by Flint, 1975; Griffen, 1977, 1982), are always perceived by women as elevations. They also raise the question of whether male activities are necessarily superior to previous activities, that is, female roles. Townsend and Carbone suggest that the data are too scanty to allow the conclusion that this transition is always a mixed blessing. In some societies, loss of fertility may mean divorce, loss of a husband's sexual interest, possibly even replacement by a new wife or concubine, while at the same time it may grant incresed respect and privilege in other social contexts. Thus, in some societies, there is a definite trade off as a woman goes from being perceived as dangerous, polluting, but sexually attractive to being perceived as asexual but with increased liberties and respect (Griffen, 1982; Townsend and Carbone, 1980). Townsend and Carbone (1980) also indicated that the taboos surrounding menstruation and female sexuality possibly represent male efforts to control female reproductive and economic behavior.

From this review of the literature, little is definitively known of the experience of menopause in non-Western cultures. Most of the literature on menopause so far has been based on the biomedical model of the Western medical system. Moreover, the current epidemiological studies on menopause indicate a discrepancy between the medical literature's portrayal of menopausal women and the way women actually experience menopause even in the West. The methodological fallacies of biomedical research on menopause and the propagation of myths about menopausal women have been addressed by Goodman (1980, 1982), Kaufert (1982),

McCrea (1983), MacPherson (1981), and others. In the Western biomedical study of menopause, only those women who seek professional help for menopausal complaints from physicians are included in the study sample. Women whose menopausal experience does not include distressing symptoms do not go to a physician for treatment. Nor would women whose cultural background provides effective nonmedical strategies for dealing with menopause be inclined to go to a physician for treatment of menopausal symptoms. The biomedical literature on menopause has created visions of a pathological syndrome that new generations of physicians are left free to presume is a scientific description of the menopausal women.

In addition, although a large body of medical and biological literature on menopause exists, no *significant* anthropological literature compares the cultural and social attitudes toward menopause of Western and non-Western societies. For example, the HRAF (Murdock, 1963) lacks ethnographic reports covering menopause, and findings related to the phenomenon are very scanty, anecdotal, inconsistent, or peripheral to other major topics of study. Menopause as a topic of study in anthropology is itself a recent development. Therefore, we know very little about the menopausal transition of women in non-Western, nonindustrialized societies with which to make comparisons with the menopausal transition of women in Western, industrialized societies.

In anthropological literature, early life has been given careful investigation: infancy, childhood, and the adult years—have all received meticulous ethnographic attention. Some authors (Griffin, 1982; Ardener, 1977) speculate that the paucity of data about menopause is related to the majority of ethnographers being male and that, male or female, ethnographers have been essentially enculturated in societies with an antiaging, antifemale bias that precludes interest in menopause. The male and female models of the world are different and the male model more closely agrees with the ethnographer's model in which economics and politics are the real subjects. Moreover, the researcher's own sex might have limited interest and access to certain kinds of information related to sexuality.

Recognizing this ethnographic vacuum, a Consensus Development Conference on Estrogen Use and Postmenopausal Women held at the National Institute of Health (NIH), September 1979, emphasized the need for intensive studies in order to understand the social and cultural factors influencing menopausal experiences. Even the few existing studies of menopause are limited because of methodological deficiencies;

nonrepresentative samples are treated as if results could be generalized to the population at large, and studies that claim to make cross-cultural comparisons are actually national studies of subgroups that share a dominant culture. To begin addressing these deficiencies, this book is designed to provide a description and interpretation of the natural history of the menopausal experiences of women in cultures that are significantly unlike that of Western industrial societies. The most striking factor in non-Western, nonindustrialized societies is the absence of hormone therapy for the physical and emotional changes said to occur among women. Also absent is the search for perpetual youth that characterizes women in the "advanced" Western societies. The findings underscore the plasticity of the human aging experience, particularly among women. The data provide answers to two basic questions: What is the social and cultural significance of menopause in traditional peasant groups such as the Mayans and the Greeks? And what are the obvious physiological manifestations of menopause among these women?

A further question, of increasing interest today, concerns the relationship of osteoporosis to menopause in non-Western, nonindustrialized societies. The assumption that menopause is necessarily linked to an increase in osteoporosis greatly strengthens the Western biomedical disease model of menopause. Yet, the expected pattern of age and menopause related bone maturation and loss may not hold for all populations and cultures (Garn, Rohnann, and Wagner, 1976; Kacyaski and Anderson, 1974; Spencer, Sagel, and Garn, 1968; Helela, 1969). One survey of the prevalence of osteoporosis in nonindustrialized cultures revealed that osteoporotic fractures are rare in these societies (Nordin, 1966). In addition to proposing genetic and environmental factors, the researcher attributed the differences to the fact that people in these cultures do not live long enough to develop osteoporosis. These studies have been too limited in number and scope to assess adequately the patterns of osteoporosis and bone loss in other cultures. The last surveys on prevalence of osteoporosis in nonindustrialized nations were conducted in 1964 (Nordin, 1966). However, recent world population data show that life expectancies for nonindustrialized nations have increased by more than 20 percent between 1960 and 1980 (World Bank, 1981). Prevalence of osteoporosis can now be examined in older, comparable populations.

Hormonal factors do not seem to explain all the variation in risk of postmenopausal osteoporotic fractures across racial and ethnic groups. No consensus is found that bone loss in older women is entirely, or even primarily, due to estrogen deficiency after menopause. Menopause is a universal natural phenomenon, but, so far, research efforts to understand its role in bone loss have been limited to samples in industrialized societies. Most studies neglect the fact that women in nonindustrialized traditional societies have different fertility patterns that might expose them to different levels of reproductive hormones, including estrogen, than in the Western, industrialized societies. Studies show that factors such as dietary intake of fat (Hill, Chan, and Cohen, 1977; MacMahon, Cole, and Brown, 1974), parity, and age at first pregnancy (Cole, Brown, and MacMahon, 1976) may alter the effective exposure to endogenous estrogens. Cross-cultural studies on the effect of estrogen on bone mass are absent and detailed research addressing this issue will contribute new insights into the study of the etiology of osteoporosis.

Research findings on the causes of and treatment for osteoporosis indicate that hormonal, genetic, dietary as well as lifestyle factors are correlates in the etiology of postmenopausal osteoporosis. A first step in tracing the relationship of osteoporosis to estrogen must involve a thorough study of all the factors noted. This work lays the groundwork for such a study by focussing on the definition and experience of menopause itself among a selected population of non-Western, nonindustrialized women. A proper understanding of the concept and experience of menopause cannot be separated from women's reproductive history as a whole, which is deeply conditioned by their whole lifestyles as women. And no matter how indirectly, women's lifestyles are radically conditioned by the overall social, political, and economic context of their lives. Therefore, this work will begin by considering the socioeconomic context of the lives of Mayan and Greek women in this study.

3

Chichimila: A Mayan Village

The Maya number in excess of two million and are the largest single group of American Indians north of Peru. They are concentrated in Mexico, Guatemala, and Belize (formerly known as British Honduras) (Vogt, 1969). They are divided into two groups: lowland and highland Maya Indians. The highland Maya are further divided into two subgroups, in Chiapas (Mexico) and in Guatemala. The lowland Maya are similarly divided into three subgroups. The first, approximately 300 people of a nearly extinct group of Lacandon Indians, live as hunters and fishermen in the Chiapas lowlands along the Guatemalan border. The second group, the Huastecs, consists of 60,000 people living in Vera Cruz and is geographically separated from the other Maya Indians. The third group, the largest single group of Mayans, are the Yucatec Maya living in Champeche, Quintana Roo, and Yucatan, who numbered approximately 500,000 in 1970 (Elmendorf, 1976). My study focussed on the lowland Yucatec Maya living in the village of Chichimila, south of Valladolid, an old colonian town, in the eastern part of Yucatan.

Background

According to the census taken by the Mexican government office in June 1981, Chichimila has a population of 2,300. It is located five kilometers south of Valladolid, about two and one-half hours by bus east of the state capital, Merida. Valladolid, with its strong Mayan influence, is a major market place for villages within a radius of 60 kilometers. The only paved

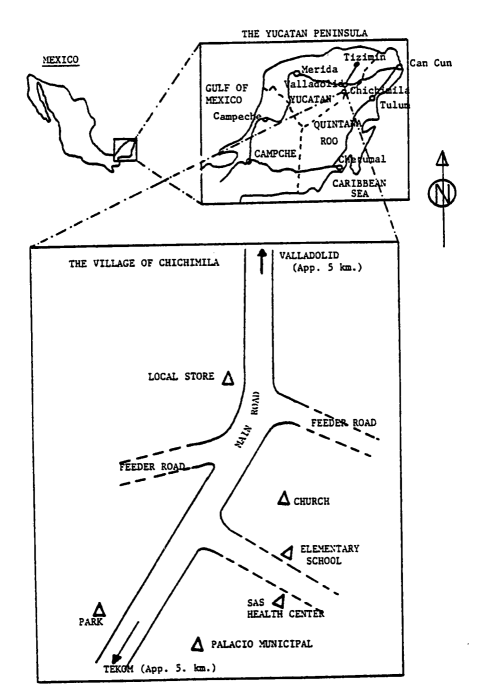

Figure 1. Map of Chichimila

street in the village is a highway that goes from Valladolid to Carillo Puerto, in the state of Quintana Roo. Four buses stop in Chichimila every day on their way from Valladolid to Chetumal. In addition, a few people who own pickup trucks and old cars make a living carrying passengers back and forth from Chichimila to Valladolid for a fare a little higher than what one pays for the bus. Chichimila has an old colonial church, an elementary school, a municipal office, a small rural clinic with no doctor, a municipal building, and a small park with a few saybo trees and flamboyant trees and benches. All of the buildings are along the highway.

Chichimila is a semitropical village. Summers are hot and humid. In May, June, and July, the temperature can reach as high as 110⁰. The rainy season begins in May. On a typical day during the rainy season there is one short downpour in the early afternoon and the rest of the day is extremely humid, with vapor rising from the ground. The dry period begins in September or October, and the temperature gradually falls until December. Midwinter evenings can be very chilly.

Two principal types of houses are found in Chichimila: the traditional thatched Mayan hut called *paja* and buildings of *manposteria*. The latter are rectangularly shaped masonry buildings, usually one room with a floor of cement or tile and a roof of wooden beams and stucco. The basic house, of whatever material, is a single room. Most of the recent construction of masonry houses has been made possible by the money earned outside the village. Houses of *manposteria* are symbols of wealth and are usually the first items in which the villagers with surplus money invest.

The majority of the people live in the *paja*, Mayan huts thatched with *juano* palms. This hut is an oval-shaped room with no windows. Both the *paja* and the masonry houses have two doors, the front door facing the path and the back door leading, in most cases, to a kitchen shack adjacent to the main house. Where a house does not have a separate kitchen, its single room provides the family's living, eating, cooking, and sleeping facilities. If a family has one or two married sons or an elderly parent living with them, it is common to find two or more houses in a courtyard or *solar*. Each *solar* is separated from adjacent ones by a low, piled stone fence. The area around the house is swept and kept free of weeds in order to keep away poisonous snakes. The average number of people living in a household is six.

A typical household has a sewing machine in a corner, a few rolled-up hammocks on the walls, a couple of stools, sometimes a chair or two, a small table in a corner and, occasionally, a transistor radio. At one corner of the room is a small bathing space divided from the rest of the room by a plastic curtain. A hole is dug into the side of the wall adjacent to the bathing place in order to let the water flow outside. The masonry houses have their bathing space in the kitchen.

All kitchen shacks, regardless of the owner's wealth, are made of mud and sticks. The kitchen usually has a three-stone hearth, low benches, gourds, pots, pans, two or three big earthen water containers; a *metate*, a concave stone slab for grinding spices; and an iron griddle, or *comal*. Near the kitchen is the *batea*, a dug-out wooden tub for washing clothes. This is usually covered with a crude thatch roof for protection from the sun. There is usually a pigpen or chicken coop or both in the *solar*; often a family will keep a couple of turkeys. Most *solares* contain one or more tin cans in which herbs and flowers are grown; these are kept on a raised shelf made of sticks out of the reach of animals. The kitchen shack is used by everyone in the household; the family's chickens and dogs are also frequent visitors, scrounging for food. Each *solar* has some variety of tree (the most common are sweet-and-sour orange, lime, avocado, mango) and a gourd plant called *jicara*. The *jicara* provides round bowls that the family use to dip water from the water container and to drink *atole*, a drink made from corn. Some *solares* have wells, but usually one well is shared by several *solares*. In Chichimila, only two households have latrines and only one house with a flush toilet.

The primary school has a latrine, and the newly built health clinic has modern plumbing, which does not work most of the time. Although the village has piped water and electricity, most of the households cannot afford to pay for these services and must use well water. Only those who live on the outskirts of the village are without electricity.

Except for a dozen individuals with Spanish surnames, the people of Chichimila are of short to medium height, with dark complexions and distinctively Mayan features. The most characteristic features of Mayans are high-bridge noses with a peculiarly curved outline and straight black hair (Shattuck, 1933). Some say that the Maya resemble Orientals, particularly the women. Indeed, in addition to having epicanthic eye folds and small stature, one of the midwives in Chichimila said that Mayan babies have the Mongolian spot referred to as *macul* or *wa* by the Maya. Villagers told me that this spot is the mark of being Maya.

More than 95 percent of the villagers have Mayan surnames, such as Tuz, Ay, Caamal, Poot, Puc, Witzil, Tun, May, Che, Chi, etc. The household survey indicates only three families with Spanish surnames,

Martin, Rejon, and Jimenez. These families acquired non-Mayan surnames from a Ladino great-grandfather or a grandfather who settled
in the village and married a Mayan woman. With the exception of the
school teachers who came from other parts of Mexico, everyone speaks
Maya in the home and streets. Although most adults and all youngsters
can speak fair to fluent Spanish, it is spoken only with visitors or officials
and in the classroom.

During the colonial era of Mexico, the term *Mestizo* identified
anyone of mixed descent. The word has acquired a unique meaning in
Yucatan: in other parts of Mexico, it is still generally used to distinguish
mixed descents from Ladinos and Indians. In Yucatan, *Mestizos* are
Mayan peasants who keep the traditions of the Indian and colonial past
and who speak Maya as their first language. *Mestizo* is also a class marker,
indicating the social position given to Maya Indians of Yucatan.
Ex-Mestizos who have denied their identification with the Maya heritage
are called *Catrins* (a Spanish word meaning "over-elegant"). These are
acculturated Mayans who have replaced the Maya folk culture with the
urban culture and have exchanged the traditional subsistence economy
for an urban lifestyle. Thus, the terms *Mestizo* and *Catrin* reflect com-
mitments to distinctive ways of life and specific values (Press, 1975) rather
than physical differences. However, the term *Ladinos* refers to the Spanish
descent of Yucatan.

Becoming a Catrin does not promote a Mayan to being a Ladino,
however. The Ladinos, Catrins, and Mestizos are separated from one
another along several social dimensions. The division of labor also
separates the two groups: the Maya are peasants, unskilled laborers, or
servants; the Ladinos are merchants, hotel owners, and professionals.
Intermarriage between Cartins and Mestizos is common; however,
intermarriage between Ladinos and Mestizos is rare.

Of the village's 2,300 residents, about 400 adult men and women
older than age 15 never went to school. Even though the rest of the adult
population claimed to have had two or more years of elementary school,
the majority of the adults do not know how to read and write. Thus,
very few adults are literate and the rest depend on their children to
mediate between them and government officials. The elementary school
in Chichimila was founded in 1939. In 1981, it had 11 teachers and 509
students. The school has eight classrooms, each with a capacity of seating
45 students. Because of shortage of space, classes are held in morning
and afternoon shifts. Class attendance is about 75 percent of the school-
age population. This is considered high when compared with other

Mayan villages. Because children are expected to help in the fields and household chores, high rates of school absenteeism are common.

With the exception of six or seven individuals, all adult women dress in the Mestizo outfit, the *huipil*, a white dress. These dresses are colorfully embroidered at the neck and hem, either by means of a sewing machine or needlepoint cross stitches in floral designs. This tunic-like dress is worn over a cotton underskirt with lace showing from beneath. Most school-aged girls also wear *huipiles*. On top of the *huipil*, the adult women wear a *rebozo*, a narrowly folded shawl. This shawl is unfolded and used to cover a woman's head when she goes to a Sunday mass or to keep her warm on a chilly evening. A few women go barefoot; otherwise, the women wear thongs or plastic sandals.

The adult men in the village, with a few exceptions, wear dungarees or polyester or gabardine slacks and sport shirts. The two specific items of clothing that distinguish a Mayan man from a non-Mayan are thonged sandals with soles made from auto tires and a soft straw hat with a wide, curving brim. In the eyes of the villagers, a man is no longer a Mestizo if he starts wearing shoes. Both men and women have special outfits for the special *jarana* dance during the annual fiesta week. The women wear *terno*, a two-piece gown, with a beautifully embroidered skirt down to the ankle, a tunic trimmed with lace, lots of jewelry, and modern high-heeled shoes. The men wear white cotton pants, white shirts, white sandals and white hats. Chichimila is one of the very few villages in which some older men still dress in what is regarded as the truly ancient Mayan manner. This includes a pair of white cotton shorts that come to the middle of the calves; over this is wrapped a cotton towel with narrow blue and white stripes. The corner of the towel is tucked in over one hip leaving an open slit at the side. Over it goes a white collarless tunic that is buttoned up at the neck and hangs loosely from the shoulders to the hips. A wide-brimmed straw hat and sandals complete the outfit.

The few people who dress differently from the rest of the villagers are called *Catrins*. For a man to be a Catrin, he must wear shoes regularly. It is also assumed that men who wear shoes will not wear white Mestizo clothing. (See also Press, 1975.) For a woman to be a Catrin, she must wear a store-bought dress from Merida or Valladolid, rather than *huipil*. The distinctive clothes of the Mestizo and Catrin reflect distinctive ways of life. The Mestizo is a *campesino*, a peasant, a *milpero*, a laborer, or a small shopkeeper. He speaks Maya as a first language. A Catrin, on the other hand, is an urban dweller. Even if he lives in the village, he does not engage in farming or exhibit the peasant lifestyle. Thus, Mestizo and Catrin are distinguished by clothing and lifestyle rather than by physical differences. It is not unusual to find quite a few people in Valladolid and also Merida who speak Maya. These are either Mestizos, who migrated to the cities thereby becoming Catrins, or Ladinos who were raised by a Mestiza servant or a nanny.

Occupations and the Village Economy

Yucatan is divided into three economic zones: the henequen zone *(Zona Henequenera)*, the maize zone *(Zona Maicera)* and the livestock zone *(Zona Ganadera)*. The maize zone has about 20 townships including Valladolid and Peto, with 200,000 people in the eastern and southeastern part of the state of Yucatan (Murguia, 1979). Chichimila is one of the villages in the maize zone, and the main occupation of the people is agriculture.

The land is flat with patches of hardened limestone and is covered with a thin layer of topsoil. Because of the nature of the land, the only method of farming is slash and burn, commonly called the *milpa* system. The bush is felled, dried, and burned, and successive crops are planted and harvested. After two or three harvests have been grown on a plot of land, it is allowed to revert to bush for a period of six to eight years before it is again cleared and planted.

The people of Chichimila grow two kinds of maize, white and yellow. Of these, the white is preferred but the yellow is more commonly grown. White maize is used for special occasions such as weddings and fiestas. In addition to maize, the villagers grow two kinds of beans, black and white. They also raise squash, tomatoes, and sweet potatoes *(camote)* at the *milpa,* which also means "farm" or in tiny fenced gardens in the *solar* (compound). Other herbs, chili peppers, and radishes are also grown in the *solar*.

Two kinds of land ownership are found in the village. One is private ownership and the other is communal ownership called *ejido.* The Mexican Constitution includes an article providing state action to regulate the use of and distribution of property, the division of large estates, the protection of small properties, and the donation of land to communities in need. To carry out these provisions, the *ejido* was created. In 1917, the Mexican Constitution designed the *ejido* program specifically to give land to deprived Indian communities. In Chichimila, out of 465 families, 160 do their *milpa* in the *ejido* system on a total of 550 hectares. One-hundred-eighty individuals own small plots of land for cultivation.

Because there is a shortage of *ejido* land in Chichimila some villagers have to rent *milpa* land from those who own relatively large plots of land. People make long trips to their *milpa,* with the average distance being about nine kilometers.

The annual agricultural cycle for the production of maize is adjusted to the climate pattern of Yucatan. The trees and bush are cut in January after the rains and allowed to dry on the ground. Burning takes place in April, after the bush is very dry and before the rains arrive. The burning requires only one day for a parcel of land. If the forest is thick, a firebreak must be cleared of brush at the boundaries to stop the fire from spreading to the adjacent properties. Throughout April and the first week of May, smoke from the burning fields fills the air of Valladolid and its vicinity. After the first rainfall in May, maize is planted. The planting is done by making a hole in the soil with a pointed planting stick. June and July are weeding seasons, and the harvest is in October. Corn is the staple food, eaten mostly as tortillas (see Chapter 6).

In addition to farming, a few families engaged in small commercial activities. Chichimila has about ten small stores where people buy salt, sugar, and other staples. The largest store is located at the entrance of the village on the right-hand side of the asphalt road as one comes from Valladolid. This store sold a variety of goods such as sardines, other food items, cooking utensils, cheap jewelry, embroidery thread and material for making *huipil,* aspirin, and tetracycline and medicinal herbs. The village has two corn mills, two butchers, and three *cantinas* (bars).

All families engage in commercial activities to varying degrees. These include sale of chickens, eggs, pigs, turkeys, tomatoes, chili peppers, and Coca Cola or bottled drinks. Two families own old pickup trucks and carry passengers to and from Valladolid. In addition, the women do embroidery and weave hammocks for sale in Valladolid.

Even though an obvious difference in wealth exists between the few entrepreneurs and the rest of the people, the villagers do not seem to recognize this as being significant. In the eyes of the villagers, they are all *campesinos,* farmers, Mestizos, and engaged in *milpa.* When I asked a few individuals who they think are the rich people in the village, they all mentioned only one person, Don Audomaro. They said that he is the only rich man because he has a big house, a bus (albeit junked in his *solar*), and educated children.

Except for having a few personal possessions such as radios and owning masonry houses, the wealthy do not differ significantly from the poor. A few *campesino Mestizo* families own transistor radios and

cassette players, especially those who have a member of the family working in Can Cun, an international resort on the seacoast. (Can Cun is
a duty-free port and Yucatecos working there occasionally smuggle con-
traband goods to the interior.) While both poor and better-off Mestizos
engage in the same activities of the *milpa* (with the exception of a few
shopkeepers) and dress similarly, the better-off Mestizos own more
changes of clothing. They eat the same kinds of foods, but the better-
off Mestizo put meat in their soup more often and buy bottled drinks
and *galletas* (hard biscuits) for their children.

As usually happens in most villages in this area, few families manage
to last the year without buying corn. Debts are generally incurred during the early summer and must be paid off after the harvest by selling
corn. This system works against the cultivators, of course. After the new
harvest is in, from October to February, villagers must sell corn at the
low price. During May and June, when the price of corn has risen,
villagers must buy it back, often from the same buyers in Valladolid.
Because no cash crop is grown in the *milpa*, the adult males usually have
to look for temporary work in the cities to earn some cash to buy items
such as clothing, sugar, and salt.

Migration

Labor migration by Chichimila men is not a modern phenomenon.
Before the opening of the tourist centers in Merida and Quintana Roo,
Mayan men used to migrate to work in the forests of Quintana Roo as
chicleros. One of the few edible wild fruits of the forested areas of Quintana Roo is the *zapote*. The *zapote* tree supplies a milky sap from which
is produced a gum called *chicle.*Enormous quantities of chicle, used as
a base for chewing gum, are exported from the eastern parts of Yucatan,
from Campeche and from Quintana Roo (Shattuck, 1933). The Maya
supplied cheap labor for collecting chicle until machines and modern
technology minimized the need for labor inputs. Today, Mayans migrate
to Can Cun, Isla Mujeres, and Cozumel, the resort areas of Quintana
Roo. They still provide cheap labor as bricklayers, gardeners, busboys,
and hotel maids.

Some Chichimileños migrate periodically between the village and
Can Cun and other localities in order to mitigate the economic hard-
ships resulting from crop failure and inflation. Other villagers go to
broaden their horizons. The men work as gardeners, bricklayers, and
busboys in the hotels and restaurants; the women work as maids and

cooks. The young men and women who commute to work in Can Cun leave the village on Monday morning, and return on Saturday. The men still maintain their *ejido* land because their main occupation is farming. A few of the young men who have semipermanent jobs in Can Cun maintain their use of the *ejido* lands by arranging with their relatives to carry on the traditional slash-and-burn agriculture in return for a share of the *milpa* harvest. This is basically an exchange constituting an urban-rural linkage within an extended family. The village relatives who are paid to work the *milpa* benefit by receiving cash for their labor as well as a share of the harvest. They are thus provided with an additional economic alternative within the village and with a means for obtaining cash without having to leave the village.

Social Organization

A Chichimila *campesino's* self-identification is Mayan, Chichimileño, and then Yucateco. He does not see himself as a Mexican, because Mexicans live in Mexico and are *huachos*, a pejorative term for mainland Mexicans. The people of Chichimila are, however, active in provincial and local elections. Chichimila is known for its people's active participation in the Caste War. In 1847, resentful of the land-hungrey Ladinos, the Mayan rebellion opened with a massacre in the town of Valladolid, the old Spanish administrative center in eastern Yucatan. This act plunged the Yucatan peninsula into one-half century of bloody civil war, called the Caste War (Reed, 1964; Ramirez, 1981). One of the Mayan leaders in the war, Manuel Antonio Ay, was from Chichimila. It was Ay's execution by the Ladinos that led to the outbreak of the Caste War. Many of his descendants, including his 80-year-old-grandson, still live in the village, and adults and young boys alike say his name with pride.

Political Organization

With the exception of one family whose sons are members of the Communist Party of Mexico and are bilingual teachers and promoters in Instituto Nacional Indiginista (INI), the people of Chichimila belong to the dominant political party of Mexico, Partido Revolucionario Instituto (PRI). Usually the party nominates one person to run for the village municipal election; however, although everyone belongs to the same party, in the last nine years, the community has been politically divided into two factions and therefore, two candidates from the same party compete with one another for the municipal office. One of the two factions is led by a teacher of Spanish descent who had been persistently running for the local office in the last three elections with no chance of winning over a Mayan opponent.

According to the villagers living around Valladolid, the people of Chichimila, as well as Kanxoc and Xocen, are quick to anger, and federal government officials are reluctant to do anything that might arouse them. The Caste War (Reed, 1964) has not been completely forgotten here, and villagers do not yet entirely trust the government. (The *campesinos* of Kanxoc have a reputation for coming to Valladolid with machetes and guns when they were angered by the government officials.) As an example of this, in November 1981, at the time of this fieldwork, Chichimila elected a new *presidente municipal.* As usual, two candidates, each supported by a different faction within the PRI (once more the persistent teacher of Spanish descent and a Mayan man) ran against each other. Both men and women vote in Chichimila and the procedure is very simple.

On the day of the election, the men stand in several rows differentiated by candidate on one side of the village's central square and the women in the same fashion on another side. Then a government official sent from Merida counts the rows and multiplies them by the number of people in each line and the winner is announced within a few minutes. The day of the election, after the vote counting was completed, members of the defeated group attacked their rivals with clubs and stones. The rioters tore down a house and destroyed two trucks that had been used by their rivals to bring voters from remote *milpas.* The police from Valladolid were unable to control the fighting and an auxiliary force was called from Merida. One of the trucks carrying policemen from Merida was overturned on the way to the village, killing one policeman and severely injuring seven others (Navidades, 1981). People started to feel at ease with each other again after the inauguration of the new *presidente* two months later.

Family Network

Each villager is tied to most of his or her fellow villagers through kinship, marriage, and fictive kinship. According to a survey done by the Mexican government in 1981, Chichimila has 465 households. A typical household consists of a husband and wife, their unmarried children, a married son, his wife and their children, and a widowed grandparent.

Very often, the households of siblings or parents and their married children share the same *solar* (courtyard).

Family members who share the same *solar* also share a single fireplace and budget, even though they sleep in separate households. Thus, when a boy marries and begins residence in the *solar* of his parents, he shares with his father all economic responsibilities and cultivation of *milpa*. A man buys clothing or personal items for his wife and children from his own earnings, but food and expensive items such as radios, tools, sewing machines, and medicines are purchased in common. As more younger sons get married and older sons purchase *solars* of their own, such sharing decreases. As parents age, each son assumes a greater share of responsibility for them. Usually, the youngest son remains in his parents' *solar* to care for them until they die. In return, he inherits his parents' house. The typical male resides within his father's *solar* during the first few years of marriage. In Chichimila, men could marry at 18 and girls at 13 or 14. In most cases, the bride lives with the husband's family. But if the bride's family does not have any sons, the groom goes to live in his father-in-law's *solar*.

Descent in Chichimila is bilateral. Individuals bear both a patronym and matronym. For a woman, marriage does not override her initial affiliation. No one refers to a married woman by other than her maiden name. Marriage is largely village endogamous and most villagers have consanguineal or affinal ties with each other.

In Chichimila, one can acquire fictive kin, *compadres*, on six occasions. The most important occasion is baptism. Tradition requires that each infant have a godfather and a godmother: the child's father is *compadre* and his mother *comadre* to the baptismal sponsors who, in turn, are *padrino*, godfather, and *madrina*, godmother, to the child. At some time before the child attains six months, generally three months for a boy and four months for a girl, a single ritual kin is acquired for a sex role ceremony called *hetzmek* (see Chapter 6). At some point before the age of seven, the child is confirmed in the Roman Catholic Church, and a sponsor of the same sex is again required. A child acquires an additional godparent when one receives First Communion. Marriage is another occasion upon which a young man or woman obtains ritual parents. As in the baptismal ceremony, both a godfather and a godmother are required. All these occasions except the *hetzmek* are rituals of the Roman Catholic Church, and all godparents except the marriage sponsors are chosen by the individual's parents. The young couple to be married usually choose their sponsors. No overlap occurs among these different sets of ritual kin.

The godparent-godchild bond is lifelong and it binds the child and his ritual parents in a reciprocal relationship. As in the ideal parent-child relationship, the child is supposed to show absolute respect and obedience toward his godparents, and the godparents on the other hand are supposed to provide moral advice and counsel for their godchild (*ahijado* or *ahijada*) and physical and economic help when necessary. If the parents of the child die, the godparents are expected to look after the child. The use of ritual kinship as both horizontal and vertical security and solidarity mechanisms has been described by Foster (1961), Davila (1971), and other ethnographers. Foster (1961) has described it as the most sacred of human ties in the Latin American peasant community.

As for horizontal versus vertical choices with respect to socioeconomic status, Foster states that vertical choices occur with much greater frequency in Latin America (1961). But in Chichimila, as in most of Yucatan, the horizontal ties are dominant. One's own parents are the most preferred godparents of one's child. Next to parents, brothers, sisters, uncles, and aunts are preferred sponsors. Very few people seek *compadres* from outside the village. Overall, the solidarity of the blood kin is more emphasized than the instrumental criterion of the social and economic status of the sponsor.

Religion

With the exception of a handful of young adults who belong to the Evangelical Church, the people of Chichimila consider themselves Roman Catholic even though most people believe in and perform Mayan rituals and cermonies. The Roman Catholic rituals and ceremonies include rosaries, novenas, masses, and processions common to Roman Catholic practice. The Yucatan Maya do not have a cargo system like the Maya of Chiapas (Vogt, 1969). Instead, each village in Yucatan has its patron saint, and each village organizes an annual fiesta in his or her honor. The patron saint of Chichimila is the "Virgen de Utrera." Its *gremio* (the ceremony performed during the fiesta sponsored by different guild members) is held in February; a fiesta open to all villagers, which includes the *corrida* (bullfight) and *jarana* (Mayan folk dance) held in March.

Chichimila has its own Catholic priest, and Mass is held almost every day. Because the priest speaks only Spanish, Mass is in Spanish. For the Maya, Mass is pure ritual. On many occasions, women are the major participants in the church ceremonies. Some of them know

"Hail Mary" and "Our Father" by heart in Spanish, but they have very little understanding of the prayers' meanings. During Mass, the priest and his Mayan helper direct the people in what to do: when to kneel, when to rise, and so on. The men's participation in church is limited mainly to the fiesta.

On the other hand, the major participants of the Evangelical faith are men. Chichimila has very few young adults who are members of this faith, and there seems to be no conflict between Catholics and Evangelicals. The Evangilical use a small masonry house that they refer to as a "temple." Evangelical preachers, unlike the villager's Catholic priest, are bilingual and communicate the scripture to the people in Maya. This denomination is supported by Evangelical churches in the United States.

Some researchers (Press, 1975; Redfield, 1934) have suggested that Maya rituals and religious traditions have survived so long because of the contribution they make to the economic life of Yucatan peasants. Slash-and-burn agriculture, with its long-term fallowing, requires extensive lands. Plots are scattered at considerable distances from population and administrative centers. Historically, the events that took place on these fields were insulated from surveillance and interference by the town-based Catholic hierarchy. Thus, Mayan ritual survived in communal- and individual-oriented form to meet the continuing needs of a specific and highly stable ecosystem. Now, after several centuries of Spanish domination, some syncretism is found between Mayan and Catholic traditions. The transmission of elements has been strictly one way, however, Mayan ritual has absorbed certain Catholic elements. For example, when the Maya *h-men*, medicine man, chants in Maya, one hears references to "Santa Cristo," "Santa Maria Virgen," and "Dios Padre" mixed with appeals to Maya deities. Although Catholic saints have been incorporated into the Mayan invocations, Mayan ritual occupies a distinctive domain of economic life, and is concerned almost exclusively with activities relating to land, weather, and crops.

In May, the *h-men* performs the *Cha Chaac* ritual to ensure rain, and all adult male villagers participate in this. In September, groups of men get together and have the *h-men* perform a ritual harvest thanksgiving called *Uhai Col*. Between September and May, no communal Maya rituals are performed. Outside of agriculture, the only interest for which the *h-men* is consulted is the prevention and treatment of sickness.

Health Beliefs and Practices

The Yucatan Maya believe that most illnesses are caused by evil winds, *mal viento*. These winds are associated with actual movements of air, malevolent supernatural beings, and certain illness symptoms. The malevolent winds are generally associated with *cenotes*, wells and caves (Redfield, 1934). Other sources of illness are *mal de ojo* (evil eye), *hechiceria* (sorcery), and the dislocation of *tipte*. *Tipte* is the central organ in Mayan ethnoanatomy; it lies just underneath the naval and is said to regulate most internal functions.

In large parts of Latin America, Mexico, and all through Hispanic and Portuguese South America, a very important explanatory element in the medical belief systems of rural people is humoral pathology, based on a notion of balance (health) and imbalance (producing disease symptoms) in "hot" and "cold" elements in the the body (Foster and Anderson, 1978; Harwood, 1971; Logan, 1973; Molony, 1975). Illnesses believed to come from cold causes are treated with hot herbal remedies, hot foods, and other hot treatments. Redfield (1934) and McCullough (1973) have described how people in Yucatan divide most foods and many herbal remedies into "hot" and "cold" categories. In Yucatan, as in other parts of Latin America, prophylactic health practices are largely devoted to maintaining proper equilibrium between these extremes.

In Chichimila, the classification of foods and diseases into "hot" and "cold" is more important to the *curanderos* (herbalists) of the bigger towns than to the villagers. In Chichimila, an important association is made between heat and *mal viento*. For example, after a woman has been cooking over a hot fire, it is thought best to wait for a while before going outside in order to avoid getting a headache. Similarly, it is believed that a person who has been walking or working in the sun should not enter a house in which there is a sick person or a newborn baby. The danger is that he will bring *mal viento* with him. In these circumstances, the person sits in the shade or in the kitchen for a while before he enters the home. Households with newborn babies always signal this fact by hanging a green plant called *anona* on the front door.

When a Chichimileño becomes ill, his or her first recourse is to try home remedies or patent medicines such as aspirin and *mejoral* (a trade name for a drug) which are available in the small stores in the village. For acute or lingering symptoms, he or she has a choice of calling a *h-men* (a traditional Mayan healer), going to a *curandero* (herbalists), seeing the nurse's aide at the rural clinic in the village, or consulting a pharmacist or a doctor in Valladolid. Most of the time, the *h-men* is chosen over a doctor because he is believed to understand the cause of most illnesses better than a doctor, and his price is affordable.

The Health Specialists in Chichimila

Chichimila has two *h-mens*, three midwives, and one nurse's aide. In many non-Western societies, the role of a curer is involuntary, something that is forced on an individual by a supernatural power, which confers on him the powers the curer will use (Foster and Anderson, 1978). In Chichimila, of the five traditional healers, the two *h-mens* and one midwife claim that they were chosen by God to perform this role, and the other two midwives stated that they chose the role from experience.

H-mens

The *h-men* is a leader or priest of traditional Mayan rituals such as the rain ceremonies (*Cha Chaac*), as well as serving as a healer (*yerbatero*). The *h-men* does not cast any evil spells on others. Of the two *h-mens*, Don Antonio is the more frequently consulted. He is 60 years old and believes that being a healer is his destiny and calling from God. He stated that his destiny is written in his palms and his knowledge of healing is God-given. He performs both preventive and curative rituals and uses herbs and prayers addressing both the Mayan deities and the Roman Catholic saints. He uses divination, exorcistic ceremonies, bathing, bleeding, and cupping. The *h-men* uses flint points or rattlesnake fangs to make incisions for bleeding; headaches, especially are treated by this method.

Don Antonio says that Tuesdays and Fridays are appropriate days for treatment of diseases. Many of the rituals performed in connection with health refer to the numbers three, seven, nine, and 13. For example, when he performed a preventive ceremony to get rid of *mal viento* from a *solar*, I saw that he used 13 stuffed tortillas, seven gourds of *posole*, and one big gourd of cooked pork and chicken. All these foods were tied to trees in the *solar* as offerings to the Mayan deities. In another ceremony, he said that the ritual requires that he walk three times around the house of the person for whom he is performing the ceremony. When I was asked to be a godmother for *hetzmek*, a Mayan ceremony performed for acknowledgement of sex roles, I had to put the child on my waist and go nine times around a table and 13 times around in the opposite direction. Don Antonio is a well-respected *h-men* and is often called to perform rituals in villages other than his own. He appears to associate every type of illness with the idea of *mal viento*.

Midwives

In Chichimila, the role of midwife requires the experience of having children. Knowledge and personal experience seem to be interdependent, and no woman without the experience of childbirth is accepted as a helper in labor. Among the three midwives in the village, two are most recognized and respected: Doña Conchita and Doña Aurora. Doña Conchita is 60 years old and, in addition to being a midwife, she has knowledge of medicinal herbs and treats women and young girls with menstrual cramps, headaches, menstrual cycle disorder, and infertility. She claims that she can ascertain the difference between a pregnant woman and nonpregnant woman by touching and examining the lower part of a woman's abdomen. She refers to this area of the body as *matriz* or womb; a pregnant woman has a "hard" *matriz*.

Doña Conchita was married at age 12. She gave birth to 13 children, six of whom are living. She started working as a midwife when she was twenty-five years old. She claims that no one taught her the skills of midwifery. God chose her to do this job and all the techniques and the herbs that she uses were explained to her in her dreams. After she gave birth to three of her own children, she started having repeated dreams of a woman telling her that she should help in labor. The woman in the dream, said Doña Conchita, was "Santa Maria." In 1979, she participated in a two-week training program given by the INI. (In 1976, INI started giving courses in Valladolid to indigenous midwives on primary care and family planning.)

Another midwife of the village, Doña Aurora is also 60 years old. She married at age 13 and subsequently gave birth to 12 children, nine of whom are living. She has been working as a midwife for 35 years. She had her first six children with a midwife but the rest without the help of anyone. She claims to have learned about midwifery from her own experience and to have started her practice by helping women in labor in her own family and her neighborhood. Doña Aurora does not give any medication or herbs to women. She only uses *sobada*, a massage given to pregnant women throughout the pregnancy period, and helps with delivery (Jordan, 1981). No one goes to her for consultation in other illnesses. She had also participated in the INI course for the *Parteras Empiricas* (traditional midwives). She was proud to show me her INI certificate and told me that she uses gloves when she checks the *matriz* during labor and cleans all her instruments in alcohol before she uses them.

Auxiliar de Salud

In addition to the *h-mens* and the midwives, the village also has a health promoter, *auxiliar de salud*, who had been trained in a 1976 three-month INI course in primary health care. The health promoter, Doña Maria, is 48 years old and was born and raised in Chichimila. She has Ladino relatives in Merida and was able to go to school in the city for a few years. Her parents recalled her to Chichimila when she was 13 years old, after completing a sixth grade education. Now she provides primary health care services in the village clinic, the *casa de salud*. She also helps the midwives with difficult births, and promotes a family planning program as part of the extension of coverage of the Mexican Ministry of Health's Maternal and Child Health Services. Her job involves keeping count of pregnant women and new born babies and treating the most frequent ailments. In return for her services she receives 500 pesos ($20.00 U. S., in 1981) per month from the government. The medicines she prescribes are available to her at cost from the clinic and she charges her patient a few more pesos over the actual cost. She restocks her supplies after reporting at a monthly meeting of health workers in the regional hospital in Valladolid.

When one has fever and acute ailments he or she is taken to Valladolid. Valladolid has six small private outpatient clinics, a small government regional hospital, a laboratory, four dentists, two pharmacies and a visiting *curandero*. The *curandero*, Don Nacho, has a room in one of the hotels permanently reserved for him. Every month he comes to Valladolid from Merida for four or five days, and people from the surrounding villages come to see him by appointment. Don Nacho has had his hotel room furnished in a style similar to the town physicians' offices.

The hospital in Valladolid is the least-used health service in the area. Even though the villagers know that they will pay less at the hospital for treatment, because it is a government service, they avoid it unless they have absolutely no money. This is because the villagers feel that the staff treats them very badly. Of the private doctors in Valladolid, the most popular one, and the practitioner who is consulted by most of the families of Chichimila is Dr. Rodriges. He is 70 years old and has been practicing medicine for 40 years in the same place.

For acute illness, the villagers prefer a doctor who will use injections. Overall, people prefer injections to pills, believing that injections cure faster. Because the town doctors want to satisfy their clients and keep them coming back, their treatment always includes an injection of antibiotics or vitamins. Health service utilization by the villager is not limited to one type of treatment at a time. A person with an acute ailment goes to a doctor in Valladolid for an injection to alleviate the symptoms but goes to the *h-men* to be cured. The *h-men* is believed to identify the causal agent and restore internal equilibrium with herbs and by performing appropriate rituals. It is understood that the treatment by the *h-men* takes time, and one must always have patience. On the other hand, if a doctor's medicine does not bring immediate results, it reflects on the doctor's ability. Sometimes a desperate mother goes to all the healers available in the area in the same day. For example, when her two-year-old adopted son got sick, Doña Blanca (the health promoter in Tekom, the closest village to Chichimila), first took him to a doctor in Valladolid. Later that same afternoon, the child appeared to be getting worse and Doña Blanca took him to a *h-men*. The next day the child was still very sick and was taken to a doctor in Merida.

Curers are classified as potentially good or dangerous. The *h-mens* and the midwives are believed to be basically good. However, the *curandero* and the *brujo* or *hechicero* (sorcerer) can harm others and are classified as potentially dangerous. A *brujo* is believed capable of assuming various animal forms, such as a dog or a cat. But in Chichimila, sorcery plays little part in the explanation of sickness or misfortune.

Types of Illnesses

Evil Eye

The villagers believe that certain people are born with the power to cause sickness (*mal de ojo*) by merely looking at others. Children and animals are thought to be the usual victims of the evil eye. The indication that a child has been affected by the evil eye is fever and green diarrhea. It is believed that evil eye can be cured only by a *h-men* or a *curandero*. The healer prays and bathes the child with water and rue (*ruda*). People in Chichimila feel that modern medicine is incapable of curing this ailment. The health promoter in the village said that her son was once sick from evil eye and a *h-men* cured him, but taking him to a doctor would have been a lost cause because modern medicine does not understand such illnesses.

Tipte

Tipte or *Firus* is an organ located just beneath the navel, and it regulates most of the internal functions of the body. Indigestion, cramp (*colicos*), vomiting, diarrhea, and menstrual problems are believed to result from the displacement of the *tipte*. It is believed that one gets *tipte* sickness when there are malevolent winds (*mal viento*): the bad wind is thought to accumulate on one's navel and to move the *tipte* from its central place. When this happens *sobada* or massage is used to put the *tipte* back in place. During pre- and postpartum massage, the midwife anchors the *tipte* in place by wrapping the abdomen with a long piece of cloth.

Preventative Rituals

The Mayan medical system is concerned with preventive as well as curative rituals. The most commonly performed preventive ritual is *kesh*, which means "change." A family needing this ceremony prepares special food (chicken and pork, pumpkin seeds, and *posole*) and invites the *h-men* to come and perform *kesh.* This ceremony is performed in order to rid one's *solar* of evil winds so that there will be harmony between the individuals in the family and good health for all (both humans and animals) who share the *solar*. The most important ceremony of *kesh* is done when a family has a child with two *remolinos* (whorls on top of one's head).

Don Antonio, the *h-men* in Chichimila, said that when a child is born with two *remolinos* the next born sibling will always be very sickly and may even die unless the parents perform the *kesh* ceremony after the child's birth. During a *kesh* for *remolinos*, the mother of the child gives the *h-men* a small chick and the *h-men* strikes the four corners of the house with the animal's head. Then, he turns the chick around the child's head (the one with the *remolinos*) nine times and with the last pass he hits the child's head with it, killing the chick with the last *golpe* (blow). Afterwards, the mother cooks the chick and the child eats all the meat; the bones are put together and buried. Before the *h-men* buries the bones, he puts a stone, covered with a piece of cloth, next to the mother and takes the child with him. With the child in his arms, the *h-men* goes three times around the parents' house. Each time he comes to the door, he asks the parents if they want to buy a child, and the mother says, "No, I already have one." The third time, the mother says, "Yes, I want to buy one because the one I had just died," and she begs the *h-men* to sell the child to her. The *h-men* sells her the child and the bones of the chick are buried, symbolizing the child's death. Now the abnormal situation is corrected through the ceremony, and the child is expected not to cause any illness in his or her younger sibling. If the family has two siblings with two *remolinos*, there is no need to perform the ceremony, because it is believed that they are equal and can resist each other's power.

Health and Hygiene from a Biomedical Perspective

A 1981 INI health survey conducted in the villages around Valladolid, of which Chichimila is one, indicated that the major illnesses in this area are parasitosis, respiratory infections (bronchitis), anemia, lack of vitamins, diarrhea, and amebiasis. Even though it was not included in the INI data, one other health problem in this area is dengue fever.

Water Supply and Waste Disposal

The major health hazard in the village is the drinking water. Underground wells are the main source of water in the village. In Chichimila, as in most villages in this area, the villagers do not give priority to building a latrine. In the entire village, only three houses have outhouses or latrines. People use their backyards and the open fields for elimination. During the rainy season all the human and animal waste is washed into the wells. Although the village pipes in water, most people can't afford the monthly payments and so they use well water. The piped water is convenient because women do not have to carry water from the neighborhood well, but the source of both the well and piped water is the same. The difference is that the piped water comes from an elevated tank, but the tank has not been cleaned for a long time and no chlorine has been added to it.

In addition to teaching family planning, the health promoter's job is to teach the villagers to boil their drinking water and to make sure that the children are vaccinated. The walls of the rural clinic are decorated with public health posters explaining the necessity of having latrines, boiling drinking water, and so on. It has been difficult to communicate to the people the importance of such issues, because these are culturally irrelevant. The health promoter herself does not follow what she teaches.

All households, those using both well water and piped water, keep their water in big earthen containers in the kitchen. The kitchen is usually a shack with no doors, and the dogs, cats, and children are always in and out, drinking from the same container. Adults and children alike dip into the water a glass or a gourd before washing it. Sometimes they wash the glass but rinse it in the main source, dip into the same water, drink some and dump the rest back into the container. Once my *comadre*, one of the women in the village most concerned with hygiene, washed the glass with soap and rinsed it in a big bucket of water and then dipped the glass into the same water and offered me a drink.

Bathing is a ritual and everyone bathes at least once a day, usually in the afternoon. They wash their clothes often and are generally meticulously clean, especially the women. However, children are allowed to play in the dirt with pigs, turkeys, and dogs. Most of the time the children younger than age five are naked, sometimes because of the family's economic situation and sometimes to avoid soiling their clothes, because toilet training is late and the child is not rushed through the training process. Often, young children who are still drinking from nursing bottles share their milk or *atole* with the household dogs. People try to keep their houses clean, but almost everyone has chickens and turkeys, wandering in and out of the house leaving their droppings everywhere. In addition to pools, standing water left by late summer rains, people keep containers of water in the *solar* for their animals. In both cases, the water is an ideal breeding place for mosquitos. During the months of September, October, and November, most people in all the Mayan villages around Valladolid, become sick from dengue fever, an acute infectious disease transmitted by mosquitos.

4

Stira: A Mountain Village in Greece

Background

Stira, the main site of the research study, is a rural Greek village on the island of Evia, the island stretching along the eastern coast of Greece, parallel to Attica (see map on page 50). Stira is three hours from Athens (two hours by bus and one hour to cross the sea). The only paved street in the village is a highway connecting the eastern and western part of the island. The closest town is Karistos on the eastern tip of the island, about 35 kilometers away. The bus from Stira to Karistos takes one hour due to the winding narrow road. Two buses stop daily in Stira on their way from Halkida (the state capital) to Karistos. The village has four cab drivers who make their living carrying passengers to and from the ferryboat station to the different villages in the area. Moreover, some young villagers own pick-up trucks and private cars. The village is built on hills, and one can see the sea (about 5 kilometers down) from most places in the village. It has a beautiful Greek Orthodox church, an elementary school, a junior high school, a court house, a police station, a post office and telephone station, a rural clinic, and a small gas station, all located around the village square called the *agora*. All the facilities except the elementary school and the clinic are shared by the adjacent villages, Kapsala and Reouzi. About five villages in the area share the same doctor.

Stira has cold, damp winters and at times it snows. In December and January, the temperature could reach 0° C. The rainy season begins

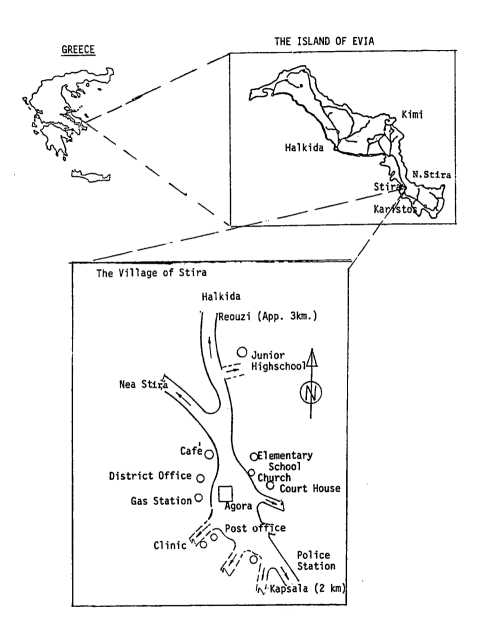

GREECE

THE ISLAND OF EVIA

Kimi

Halkida

N.Stira

Stira

Karysto

The Village of Stira

Halkida

Reouzi (App. 3km.)

Junior Highschool

N

Nea Stira

Café

Elementary School

District Office

Church

Gas Station

Court House

Agora

Post office

Clinic

Police Station

Kapsala (2 km)

Figure 2. Map of Stira

in March and lasts through May. Summers are hot but the evenings are breezy. The summer season is from June through September, and the temperature starts falling around the end of September. Because the village is on the narrow neck of the island, it is known for being windy all year. In summer, the wind brings cool breezes, but in winter it makes life in the village difficult. Several times during winter, strong winds leave the village without electricity, telephone, and transportation (ferryboat). Winter nights are very cold and so damp that clothing and the bedding feel wet.

All houses in Stira are built from brick and cement and are usually two stories, connected by outside stairs. Some houses have a veranda and most have stone walls about one foot high and six inches thick and white washed. A typical house has a living room, kitchen, and bedroom on the first floor. The ground floor is used as a store room and a stable if there is no other building for the animals. A typical store room is used to keep farm implements, cheese, oil, barrels of wine, and a bin of cereals such as corn, wheat, and oats. In the back yard of the house, one finds a chicken coop, a winter shelter and feed for the sheep and goats, and · a brick oven. In addition, most houses have a barn in which the hay and straw are kept. The barn is usually a single room made of bricks located at the edge or outside of the compound. Most houses have flush toilets and running water. However, some houses have latrines.

A typical living room in the village is furnished with some arm-chairs, in some cases a sofa, a long table covered with an embroidered tablecloth and a plastic cover to protect the cloth, and the whole room is decorated with the best embroidery and crafts made by the women of the family. Pictures of the family members are hung on the walls. This room is usually kept closed, and it is used only on special occasions such as on a nameday of a family member, when guests come to visit, and on Christmas and Easter. In winter, the living room floor is covered with rugs or rag rugs, which the women make on the looms with dyed sheep wool or with strips of old clothes that they cut up when they no longer are wearable. There are one or two bedrooms (depending on the family's size) and a kitchen. For the most part, the bedding (sheets and blankets) are woven by the women, and the pillows cases are embroidered. The kitchen, which is also the family room, has a sink and cold running water, a gas burner, a table, a few stools, and chairs. This room also has a low single bed or a wide bench covered with blankets. On the wall there is a small cupboard where the dishes, knives, forks, spoons, and glasses are kept. Some of the pots and pans are hung on the wall. This room also has a large fireplace; the family uses this room to cook, eat, and keep themselves warm. The fire burns all winter in this room, except when the house is empty or at night. At times, the fire is used for cooking. In addition to the fireplace, some families have a wood stove for cooking and warmth; others have a gas burning heater. The kitchen is the room in which all daytime work is conducted, and, because it is the warmest room in the house, an elderly person in the family usually sleeps here. Most households have a television and a telephone. In the kitchen or one of the other rooms, each household has a small shelf high on the eastern corner of the wall with icons of the family's favorite saints, an icon of Virgin Mary, and the sanctuary lamp hanging in front. The lamp burns continually. Every Saturday, the evenings before a saint's day, and holidays the women of the family change the oil. The average household has four or five residents; a husband and his wife, two children and a grandparent (usually the husband's mother or father).

The people of Stira claim that their ancestors came from Albania before the conquest of Greece by the Turks and call themselves *Arvanites*. Greek is the main language spoken by everyone in the village, although some families speak a dialect called *Arvanitika* at home. The Arvanites are spread in northern, central, and southern Greece. However, only the residents of Evia still continue to use Arvanitika. Other than this, the people of Stira are no different from any small farming community in Greece. The most common family names in the village are Sakkas, Zappas, Tolia, Peppa, Lewoni, Tountas, Revithi, and so on. My survey indicated that out of 800 people (450 in Stira and 350 in Kapsala) about 62 adults, age 40 to 98, have never been to school. The rest of the population claimed to have had some years of elementary school and some young adult males claimed to have had completed junior high.

Apart from the house and its furnishing, the most important item that indicates a family's degree of modernity in Stira is clothing. No one wears the traditional outfit anymore. Traditional regional clothing, the short white pleated skirts for the men and the long dresses with embroidered vests for women, are now worn only by the school children in the parades and plays presented on patriotic occasions in March.

Men wear the standard European-style suit, shirt, socks, and shoes. The older men avoid wearing ties even on special occasions; however, some of the young and middle-aged men wear ties on holidays and special occasions. While working out in the field, the older men wear heavy wool trousers, sweaters, and wool caps.

The women's clothing patterns vary slightly based on age as well as income. The older women, age 60 and older, wear dark blue, gray, or brown. Widows wear black the rest of their lives. The older women always wear loose dresses, button down with long sleeves, long stockings, cloth slippers, and woolen shawls. They wear black or brown scarves wrapped around their heads, necks, and mouths, with ends tied on the top of their heads. Underneath the scarves, their hair is dressed in braids around their heads. In Stira, the young women wear yellow and black scarves when working in the field. This black on yellow design is a regional color of eastern Evia. Women in the other parts of the island wear black on white or black on purple. The oldest women and the least prosperous middle-aged women dress the same at all times, even holidays. The rest of the women dress in the standard European outfits, dresses or two-piece suits, on Sundays when they go to church and on holidays. Most women own sewing machines and they make beautiful outfits for themselves and their children.

Occupations and the Village Economy

The main occupation of the people is agriculture. The land is rugged and hilly. Thus, the main method of farming is terracing, except in the valley. They use mules and horses for plowing and most people have small plots of land scattered in different parts of the village. The major crops are wheat, barley, corn, grapes, olives, vegetables, and fruit, all of which (except for olives) are strictly for household consumption. They also grow clover for animal feed. In late October and early November, the farmers plow the plots to be sown with winter wheat. After plowing, the seeds are sown by hand. Each farmer devotes a small area of land to growing grapes. Wine is made for consumption at home. In the middle of February or beginning of March, depending on how bad the winter was, they start pruning the grape vines. During this time, vegetables are planted. The people in Stira grow tomatoes, spinach, lettuce, fava beans, green beans, artichokes, zuccini, eggplant, and onions. Throughout spring and summer, the vegetables need to be watered, weeded, and picked. In April and May, the wheat is harvested; in the fall, the olives are picked. Olive picking requires every family members' participation because it is a time-consuming job and should be finished before it gets very cold.

In addition, most people own some chickens, sheep, and goats. The ones who own big herds make extra income by selling lambs and goats to the people in the big towns. Especially at Eastertime, a lot of people come to the village to buy their Easter lamb. The milk from the sheep and goats is used to make feta cheese and yogurt for household consumption. Only two families raise pigs as an occupation. Each household also owns a horse, donkey or mule. The horses and mules are used to pull the plow in the field. Together with the donkeys, the horses and mules carry heavy loads to and from the field. The farmers also ride these animals to and from the farm and between villages. Side saddle is the normal riding position for both men and women.

Land is privately owned. In Greek society, property is transferred from one generation to the next through dowries and inheritances. Greek laws of inheritance require that property be divided equally among all children. However, the daughters of a family are entitled to their share at marriage in the form of dowry. Because a man's most important obligation is to make sure that his daughters are successfully married, in Greek society the girls have priority on the family's property. In a farming community like Stira, land is very valuable and therefore dowries are calculated on a transfer of land from the family to the daughter and then through her to her husband. In most cases, sons of the family do not get married until their sisters are all married. Because of the dowry and inheritance system, farmland in Stira is divided into small plots and scattered all over. In families where there are more daughters than sons, there may not be enough plots of land left for the sons. One way villagers try to solve this problem is by training or educating the sons for non-farming occupations. In addition, the urban lifestyle is highly prized by villagers. Families make an effort to get their daughters married to urban dwellers as well as sending their sons to the big towns and cities for their educations.

Besides farming, some families own a small business in the village. Stira has four small stores where people get rice, salt, sugar, and canned goods; a mill where the wheat is ground and the olives pressed; three butchers; four tavernas and four coffee houses. The tavernas function every evening in summer and only weekend nights in winter. Most families engage in some business activities. For instance, in the summer, the surplus vegetables are brought to the agora (the village square) on a mule or donkey and are sold. Some women sew for a fee. In one household, the man owns a truck and makes a trip to Athens once a week to bring merchandise for the shopkeepers in the villages. Stira also has four cab drivers who run people back and forth from the ferryboat and to the different villages. Other than the school teachers, doctor,

policeman, and two men working in the post office, who are all outsiders, the rest of the people in the village are farmers.

There is variation in the wealth and the amount of land a family
owns and the income each household generates outside of farming. Those
who own the pig farms, the butcher stores, and the *tavernas* earn a
relatively substantial income. These families own private cars, send their
children to schools in Athens, and the wives and children are always
well-dressed with the latest fashion in Athens. Moreover, unlike the other
women in the village, these women do not work in the fields.

Migration

Historically, Greece has experienced a great deal of internal and exter-
nal migration. Wars such as World War II, the Civil War, and the war
with the Turks created a people used to moving either because they were
displaced or because the wars took them away from their villages.
Another factor is that many Greeks seek temporary employment in West
German factories or go to Australia or the United States to work, because
for some time these countries have asked for the unskilled labor that
Greek immigrants can provide (McNall, 1974). All these conditions are
related to economic problems in the villages caused by crop failures and
depression. Most Greek emigrants are from small villages of the Greek
islands, and Stira is no exception. In Stira, some households have sons
or close kin in Germany, Australia, South Africa, and the United States.
Three families that I know in the village have brothers in Detroit,
Michigan; the priest of the village had a younger brother in New York;
three men in the village said that they had lived and worked in the United
States between eight and ten years, and they now are engaged in farming.

In Stira, as it is in most Greek villages its size, the villagers admire
and try to emulate the standard of living that exists in big towns and
cities. Their knowledge of these standards is acquired through first-hand
information brought back by their children and relatives, by personal
visits to the urban areas, and, in the last few years, through television.
The village is losing its young to the urban areas. For instance, the young
boys who finished junior high feel that no opportunities exist for them
in the village. Education is highly prized, and most families send their
boys for further training to Halkida or Karistos on the island or to Athens.
Even though the schools in Greece are free, the family must pay for rooms,
board, and school supplies. Most of the time, the child boards with a
relative in the city, and the parents pay fees to the relatives to cover the

cost of their child's care. Even though the young girls in the village are not encouraged to continue their education away from home, they too want to marry someone from a big town and live in the physical ease and comfort that they think the urban life will provide.

This type of mobility is leaving many villages abandoned by the young. Stira, like most other Greek farm villages, has more older people, 60 years old and older than young adults. Very few young couples reside in the village; for example, the elementary school had only 25 children, and the year that this study was done, there was only one child in the first grade. Throughout my field work, I saw no weddings or baptisms in the village.

In the past, children looked after their aged parents. The youngest son always stayed with his parents. When he got married he brought his wife home to stay with the family. He took care of the family and when they died he took over the house and property in return. Nowadays, some anxiety and fear is associated with aging. Parents worry that when they get old, no one will be there to look after them and their farms; at the same time, however, they want their children to have a better life than the village can provide. Most elderly, rural Greeks are faced with the dilemma of looking after themselves. This is already happening in the village; most old people live alone. Their children usually come to visit on holidays and occasionally send them money. Some have had telephones installed to enable them to check on their parents.

An 80-year-old woman told me her son calls almost every day to see how she is, and he also bought her a television so that she would not feel lonely. A 94-year-old woman said that her children have "dropped her like a dirty stick," and they do not care for her. She cooked for herself, and gathered wood for winter, and did every thing except washing, which her neighbors did for her. This woman died shortly after I met her, and her children were criticized by the villagers for not caring for their mother.

Housing in the cities is hard to find. Most people could afford only a one bedroom apartment even with two or more children; those with a widowed parent have an additional problem. Moreover, old people generally do not like the city. They are used to the village life where they have friends and relatives. Most elderly people in Stira said that they can take the city only for a day or two. Thus, even if their children have space, the older people are not willing to leave their village lifestyle to be cooped up in a small, city apartment. Unless some young people decide to return to the village, Stira will become another dying Greek village.

Social Organization

In Greece, when two adjacent villages do not meet the minimum population of a commune, that is, 500 residents, they are classified as being in the same commune by the central government as are Stira and Kapsala. These two villages jointly elect a village council, *proedros*, with representatives from both villages, and share the same secretary. The main office of the council is in Stira. The third village, Reouzi, is classified in another commune and has a different council. In November 1982, it was election time for new mayors and councils in all the cities and villages. The Greek political structure has three parties: the New Democratic Party, the Socialist Party, and the Communist Party. Stira had two political parties in its 1982 local election. The candidate from the New Democratic Party, who was also the incumbent, won the election. The most important responsibility of the village council is the preparation of tax rolls. Because taxes are based on land tenure, produce, and livestock ownership, the council must prepare lists of what each villager owns.

The village also has a police station with two policemen and a court house. Stira is the only one in the area with a court, but the judges and the councils who determine one's fate all come from Halkida. Overall, the people are skeptical of any government official and believe that juries can be manipulated with money.

Family Network

In the Greek community, the nuclear family is the most important economic unit. It is also a unit that determines the family's honor or shame. Thus, each individual's action reflects on the family's self-esteem, and the family always protects its members from outsiders. The villagers' closest kin are their nuclear family; the extended family consists of first and second aunts, uncles, and cousins. They also acquire affinal and spiritual kin during their lifetimes. In Stira, the immediate families, or elementary groups, do not live in a joint, cooperative household. Giving newly married couples property and dowries serves as a mechanism to separate the newly wed couples structurally from either set of parents. Through marriage, one takes on the whole of his or her spouse's kin, and the close kin of the one become the kin of the other and are referred to in the same terms. However, a real confidence and trust exist only with people of the same blood. Therefore, relations between affines are by courtesy rather than mutual trust.

The individual also acquires spiritual kin when he or she is bap-
tized or married. Usually, the godparent for one's child is chosen by the
parents outside of the blood kin. The godparent is *nona* or *nonos* to
the child and *kumbara* or *kumbaros* to the parents. The term *kumbaros*
is used for both marriage and baptismal sponsors. Because the term *kumbaros* is considered part of the system of kinship terminology, it imposes
prohibition against marriage in the same degree as those given to blood
relatives. Just as a family chooses a marriage partner for their child, they
try to find *kumbaros* whose wealth and position will be source of potential
help for themselves and their child. Moreover, because the *kumbaros*
is not related, he or she is more likely to be from outside of the village,
in the big towns or cities, and usually inequality in the wealth and social
positions exists between the villagers and their *kumbaros*. The villager
usually chooses a prosperous farmer or an urban merchant, someone
economically better than himself. The villager establishes different types
of relationships with individuals outside of his immediate family; fulfill-
ment of obligations are reciprocal but not necessarily identical.

Religion

In Stira, everybody belongs to the Greek Orthodox Church. The affairs
of the church in the village are administered by the priest with the help
of a committee of four. Income for the church is derived from the Sunday collections, sale of candles, and rental of church property. The priest
receives a salary from the Greek government. In Stira, the priest is very
influential. He is a native of the village and is in his seventies. Before
becoming a priest, he used to be a truck driver. He is married and has
one daughter who is married and lives in Athens. He is well-respected
and loved, and his temper is also tolerated. Sometimes he interrupts the
liturgy and shouts at people, especially at women who seem to gossip
in church. There is liturgy every Sunday morning and holidays. People
put on their best clothes when they go to church, making the Sunday
liturgy a village "show-and-tell" of the latest dress styles.

Most Greek villages have annual fiestas called *panigiri* for the patron
saint of the village. However, Stira had not held such a fiesta for the
last two years because the council felt that there were not enought people
to carry out the event. Besides the big Easter and Christmas holidays,
the village does not organize carnivals and *panigiries* like other villages
its size. Easter is the most well-attended religious holiday, and most city
dwellers spend this holiday with their families and relatives in the villages.

Health Beliefs and Practices

In Greek rural culture, people believe that illnesses are caused by different agents and that each illness has its own cure. Thus, in Stira, people believe that illnesses such as evil eye and spirit possession are caused by supernatural power and that illnesses such as the common cold, rheumatism, indigestion, and *afalos* (dislocation of the navel) are believed to be consequences of natural phenomena such as cold weather, hard work, distress, or bad food. Moreover, the villagers have some awareness of contagious diseases such as tuberculosis and childhood diseases, and they take steps to protect themselves and their children by having the necessary vaccines.

Stira has a rural doctor and a small outpatient clinic. The Greek government appoints new medical school graduates to different rural areas for a one-year national health service. Even though the villagers are familiar with modern medicine and have access to free medical service, the most common healing methods are home remedies. When home remedies fail, the medical doctor is then the most frequently used health resource. People respect the physician and his skills. However, the continuation of patterns of local healing culture indicates the vitality and strength of the old traditions in curing diseases. Stira does not have a specialized practical healer as do other villages. Most of the time, the traditional healing is performed by an older woman of the family or in the neighborhood. Occasionally, the priest performs some curative rituals. The most frequently used home remedies are herbs and spices such as camomile tea, mountain tea, mint, sage, oregano, and marjoram; liquors such as ouzo, cognac, and *tzipouro* (a strong home made liquor made from distilled grape seeds); divination called *xemetrima*; spring water and oil from a shrine; rubbing; and cupping. Until very recently, the villagers used poppy leaves, *paparuna*, for insomnia, and to calm down a crying baby. However, about three years before this research was undertaken, government officials from Athens came to the village, pulled the roots of this plant in the village, and informed the villagers about the dangers of using poppy plants. While poppies still grow wild in the mountain side, people have stopped using them as medicinal herb. Some people said that they used to put the leaves of poppy plants in their spinach pies.

The villagers employ the various treatments available simultaneously. Thus, frequent use of home remedies does not negate visits to the doctor and vice versa. However, people generally see a doctor only after the illness has become very serious. One of the reasons is the fear that the doctor will ask them to give up some working days or ask them to decrease their work activities. For some people, the daily work needed in a peasant lifestyle makes taking time out from their daily routines impossible. A man is unwilling to leave his work in the field to attend a lingering ailment; a woman finds it very difficult to leave her household in order to see a specialist in Athens or Halkida. The children and the animals need her constant attention, and she will try every home remedy before she goes to a doctor for diagnosis. Out of fear, some people deny pain and put off going to a physician if they suspect a severe illness. For example, one of the young truck drivers in the village, a family man of 43 had fever on and off, at times as high as 40° C. However, because this was the time the men prepare their plots of land for winter wheat, going to the doctor meant taking time off from his farm work and his routine of driving to Athens twice each week to bring goods to the village shops. He avoided seeking help until he was completely unable to function. After having dry cough and fever for a couple of weeks, he became very sick, and his wife called the village doctor. He was diagnosed as having pneumonia, had to remain in bed for several days, and hire someone else to finish his farm work before the season for sowing winter wheat was ended.

People seem to have a high tolerance for pain and discomfort, especially the women. One of the women in the study sample had her uterus collapse ten years ago when she had her last child, and she still had not been to the doctor because she feared the inconvenience her going to Athens might cause her family. Every season there is work that must be done. She might have had time during the winter, but her children had school and she felt she cold not leave them alone. In summer, the children were at home, but then the farm work needed her attention. Consequently, she is waiting until all her children grow up so she will have time to take care of herself. In general, villagers feel any treatment other than home remedies disturbs their activities, takes time out from urgent work, and may be expensive. Moreover, villagers are fearful of what the doctor will find wrong with them. They are not anxious to go to a big city where they are treated badly by hospital staff who, they have heard or experienced in the past, look down on unsophisticated and poor people from the country. One woman, who had her last child in a hospital in Karistos, said that she cried most of the time during her three days stay in the hospital because the staff were unsympathetic, and she felt lonesome.

The rural doctor in the village usually gives primary care. Anything that needs an x-ray or laboratory work is referred to Athens or to nearby cities. He is also responsible for the other five villages in the area and rotates his time serving each village. During the winter, the doctor sees many people with colds and flu. During holidays and summer, most people are taken ill from eating too much or from food poisoning. He also makes home visits for older patient who are unable to visit the clinic. High blood pressure is common among the older people in Stira; therefore, he takes their blood pressure and makes sure that they follow the medication prescribed for them by a physician in Athens.

The villagers do not see any contradiction in their simultaneous use of herbs and modern patent medicine. They believe that one is not harmed by herbs. Furthermore, they believe that diseases have various causes, each of which has its own cure. For example, they do not believe that the doctor could cure such illnesses as evil eye, *afalos*, and *xrisi* (jaundice).

Evil Eye

The belief in evil eye is common in most non-Western countries and throughout the Mediterranean world. This is an ancient belief that attributes magical power to the human eye. However, the treatment of this illness varies among cultures. The harmful effect of the evil eye is believed to occur without any intent on the part of the beholder. He is believed to be born with this power and often is not aware of any special power within his eyes. The power is explained by the villagers as being magnetic or a result of admiration or envy of what another person has and the person with the evil eye does not. Because villagers believe that anyone can have the evil eye, they spit symbolically every time they admire new objects, a child, or animals, and say, "Tuf, tuf, na min se matiazo." ("Tuf, tuf so that I don't harm you with my eyes.") A person with evil eye is believed to affect a baby, a well-dressed adult, an animal, or an object such as a car. Moreover, this person need not have any special relations to the person affected by his power. Therefore, a mother could bewitch her own baby or a man his own horse or sheep.

The effects of evil eye vary from discomfort such as headache, dizziness, and vomiting to sudden death. Usually, sudden death is believed to happen to children and animals. Evil eye is usually treated by an older woman in the family or in the neighborhood. An older woman who knows how to cure this illness uses a cup of water with a drop of oil in it. Then she starts her divination, *xemetrima*, by calling for help from her favorite saints and makes the signs of the cross several times on the sick person and the cup of water and oil. After saying her healing words to herself so that no one else hears them, she starts yawning and her eyes get tearful. In the meantime, the oil disintegrates in the water. The disintegration of the oil and her yawning are evidence that the person had been affected by evil eye. After this process, the sick person is expected to feel better. If the process is used for an animal, then the healer uses salt and water, says her *xemetrima*, and sprinkles the mixture on the animal. I was told that the bewitched animal usually gets up on its feet after this healing process.

The technique of curing evil eye is inherited or stolen from another healer. Because stealing the words of the *xemetrima* without the healer's knowledge is believed to be more effective, and also strips the healer of any such power, most older women do not say the words aloud. They just mumble to themselves. The healer passes this knowledge to a good friend or close family member before he or she dies. This is knowledge that a mother-in-law passes to her daughter-in-law. Once the healer tells the words to another person she loses her power to cure. Some villagers have rue planted in front of their houses to ward off the power of any possible person with evil eye. The same plant is used in Ethiopia and Yucatan for the identical purpose. In the case of Yucatan Maya, the person affected is bathed with water and rue.

Some of the other illnesses that the villagers believe modern medicine does not cure are *afalos* and *xrisi*. *Afalos* is the movement of the naval from its place due to lifting heavy loads, causing all sorts of illnesses such as vomiting, stomach aches, and nausea. The navel is believed to move from its place and goes as far as the arm pit or to the back of the body. A woman or a man who knows how to cure this ailment returns the navel to its place by massaging it carefully.

Xrisi (jaundice) was explained to me as an illness that makes the sick person's eyes and skin yellow. This is cured by cutting the membrane connecting the inside of the upper lip to the gum. I was told this illness is not common in the village any longer. However, most adults claimed they had *xrisi* when they were young.

Even though most of the family healers are women, a few mentioned their husbands as main healers in the household. An old women in Stira is likely to have a variety of healing skills. The healing practice ranges from the exchange of advice among village women about which herb to use for stomach pains or common colds to *xemetrima* for evil eye to a visit to a physician. Information about herbs and healing techniques is freely communicated among the villagers, with an only exception being *xemetrima* for evil eye. A traditional healer is not set apart from others. The healer charges no fee or requires no gifts. For example, a woman healer is acknowledged for her skills and she does what she can to help others without competing with the physician for money. She herself probably has used physicians for ailments believed best cured by modern medicine. The selection of treatment for an illness is based on what the family thinks the cause of the illness could be.

A woman usually acquires such skills as home remedies and the use of herbs from her mother, mother-in-law, grandmother, or, occasionally, from someone outside of the family. The healing power could be learned through observation or through stealing the words of the *xemetrima*. If an older healer wants to pass on the words of the *xemetrima* to a younger member of the family or to someone else, the healer says the words out loud so the younger person can overhear and learn them.

Besides the family healers and physicians, the villagers also refer to the priest as a healer. People go to a famous priest, a shrine, or a church to be cured from illnesses. Holy water and holy oil from the church are used to treat ailments. People also invite the priest to come to their houses at the beginning of each month to bless the houses. This blessing is believed to rid evil spirits and any misfortune from them. In Stira, after the priest suffered a heart attack, he was unable to walk up and down the hills visiting every household, and villagers were concerned about the decrease of his services.

Overall, sorcery did not seem to be a concern as a source of health problems in Stira. People felt that black magic and sorcery are performed by gypsies, and no gypsies live in the village or nearby, although some live on other parts of the island. They also did not use the technique of divination called *fingani*, which most Greek peasant women use to predict the future by looking at the arrangements of the coffee sediments from a cup used to drink the thick Turkish coffee. This act is condemned by the Greek Orthodox Church, and the women of Stira claimed they never practiced such acts.

The knowledge of home remedies and the art of practical healers once extensive in the village is now gradually dying as young people leave the villages and the value of modern medicine dominates the traditional methods. For example, the art of traditional midwifery had died in Stira a long time ago. The village had two well-known midwives, but no one took up the practice after them. For a long time, the village had a native physician and a trained midwife who travelled by horseback, delivering babies at home. Because the physician died and the midwife was no longer available, when a pregnant woman approaches her delivery day, she generally stays with relatives in Athens (or the city where she planned to have her baby) until she delivers. If an error had been made with regard to the due date or if labor started earlier than the time anticipated, she would be rushed by taxi to the nearest city with hospitals. I was told that a few years ago, a taxi driver helped a woman deliver in his car while crossing on a ferryboat to a clinic in Athens. This type of accident is not a major concern for the villagers because few young couples live in the village. The rural doctor in Stira said that in his four years service in the village he had never dealt with a pregnant woman for prenatal care or delivery.

Cleanliness and Hygiene

Most houses in Stira and adjacent villages have sanitary facilities. The majority have inside plumbing and flush toilets. A few who did not have such facilities have latrines. The indoor plumbing and the flush toilets are new improvements achieved within the last ten years. The house is the domain of the women, and the status of good village housewife requires considerable time and energy on the maintenance of home cleanliness. The people value cleanliness and order. The furniture in the house and the kitchen is kept in its proper place. Pots and pans are hung on a wall or kept in a cupboard. Clothes are kept in a closet or big metal or wooden cases. Every morning a woman takes all the bedding out in the air for a couple of hours before she makes the bed, sweeps the floors and dusts the rugs. (The bedding must be aired out every morning due to the dampness in the house, especially during the winter season.) Such orderliness applies also to the storeroom where farm equipment is kept. Each spring, with the help of her husband, a woman takes all rugs to a village spring to wash and pound the heavy rugs; when they are dry she then stores them until winter. Before Easter, the entire house (including the steps and the terrace) is whitewashed. In Stira, villagers criticize a woman who does not keep a clean and orderly house. Among all the households I visited, I saw only one house that was unclean, with a haphazard collection of garments and utensils.

People bathe and wash their clothes often. Work clothes used in the field are kept separate from the everyday wardrobe. The kitchen utensils, drinking glasses, and dishes are kept clean. Most of the time, women do not have the need to keep containers of water because they have a sink and running water in the kitchen. The only time villagers must keep water in containers is during summer, when the village water supply is reduced to two or three hours of service due to a lack of rain. During this time, the water is kept in plastic containers with lids.

The villagers are unaware of dental hygiene. They are used to eating sweets in different forms, from cookies to preserved fruit. In addition, an adult villager drinks three to four cups of very sweet Turkish coffee daily. The habit of brushing one's teeth is known to a very few individuals; consequently, the majority of the villagers have bad teeth and gums.

5

Getting to Know the Women

Entrance to the Community and Establishing a Network in Chichimila

As stated in Chapter 3, the work in Yucatan concentrated in the Mayan villages around Valladolid, one of the old colonial administrative centers situated in the eastern part of the state, halfway between Merida and Can Cun (see map on page 28). The villages in the Valladolid area are very traditional. The people are subsistence farmers who speak mainly Maya. They still practice the traditional Mayan ceremonies, and the majority of the women and the men still wear the traditional Mestizo outfits reflecting a commitment to traditional Mayan cultures and strong identification as Mayan.

After visiting several villages in the area, I selected the village of Chichimila as the focus of the research for the following reasons: Chichimila is very traditional yet the population is large enough to ensure a numerically significant sample size for the study. In addition, it has a small rural clinic that I was able to use as a base. Such clinics are common in villages the size of Chichimila. Moreover, I had several helpful contacts. A physician friend, who is a native of the village and works for INI, was able to introduce me to key people, including a nurse's aide who is a native of Chichimila and speaks both Maya and Spanish, the mayor, and the priest of the village who helped facilitate my entrance to the community.

Mayan women are very shy and use the Maya language as a barrier to outsiders. During my first few weeks in Chichimila, my presence was generally ignored by the local women. My greetings on the street were never returned; women usually pulled their shawls, *rebozo*, over their heads and passed by quickly. At first, most of my contact with the women of Chichimila was at the rural clinic, where I asked women who had come for treatment to meet with me later. They all politely said they would come, but no one did.

I also went to church every Sunday because most women attend Mass then. After a few discouraging attempts to hold a meeting with the women, I asked the priest if he could speak about me in church after Mass. One Sunday, the priest called me to come to the altar after the Mass was over and, with the help of an elderly woman who spoke Maya and Spanish, announced to the people who I was, where I came from, and asked them to cooperate with me and to attend at least one meeting with me. After the priest was finished, I announced the day and time of the next meeting and thanked them in the only Mayan words I knew at the time. I saw people smiling and sensed that they were happy to hear me say something in their own language.

The next day, a few women and their husbands came to my meeting at the rural clinic. I explained to them I was there to learn about their culture, especially the lifestyle of the women, and that I would like the women of Chichimila to teach me. They did not seem to understand what I meant because they were accustomed to outsiders coming to teach them or their children, or to doctors or nurses sent to vaccinate their children. Because my first introduction to the village was through a native physician from INI, the villagers assumed that I was also a physician. This was the first time a stranger had come to learn about their culture, and they wanted more explanations. The women started asking me about my cooking ability and other aspects of their notion of a female roles. They discovered that I had fewer skills than a seven-year-old girl in the village and definitely needed training. Initially a few women volunteered to start teaching me how to make tortillas and *huipil*. From that day forward, I became a student, and women in the village took an interest in me, teaching me how to cook and allowing me to participate in their everyday activities.

My first lesson was at the household of Dona Blandina and Don Lorenzo, where I was taught to make tortillas and bean soup. It was easy to make the soup but I had a hard time making the tortilla perfectly round. It seemed effortless when the women did it, but my tortilla had to be inspected by the mother of the house and reshaped before it was put on the grill to cook. While I was learning to cook, I was watched by the neighbors' children who were seven to ten years old. Because this was a task a seven-year-old girl performs with a perfect ease, they were shocked to see my lack of coordination and could not help laughing. In their limited scope, the villagers assumed the rest of the world ate tortillas, and they could not imagine a mother who would permit me to leave home without having taught me the simple skill of tortilla making.

I continued such apprenticeships in cooking, embroidery, and weaving hammocks until I left the village. This relationship allowed me to get to know the women within their households and engage in conversations on different topics related to my research. Concomitantly, it gave the villagers opportunities to learn about me. They were curious about where my family was and how my mother allowed me to leave home. When I told one of the women that my mother died when I was very young, she was heartbroken and with tears in her eyes she said, "That is why you left home. If you had a mother, she would not have allowed you to go far from her." She said that as long as I stayed in Chichimila, she would be my mother, and indeed she took me in as one of her daughters. She saved a portion of food every time she cooked a special dish. For the annual village fiesta *jarana* dance, she dressed me as a Mestiza in the traditional *terno* outfit with the rest of her daughters. She even tried to teach me how to dance, although I never got the steps quite right.

The people were kind and sympathetic, and their houses were always open to me. The majority of the women had never left the village except for occasional trips to Valladolid, and it was difficult to explain to them how far Ethiopia was from their village. Some men thought Ethiopia was a *pueblo* (village) in Merida, others thought it was in Mexico. Because everyone had heard of Jerusalem in connection with the Catholic religion and were aware of the fact that it is very far from Mexico, I finally decided to use Jerusalem as reference point for distance. I really did not think that they understood how far it was, but I was satisfied to have found a reference point telling them that my home was beyond Jerusalem.

Offering and accepting food is a sign of friendship in the Maya culture. I ate everything that I was offered. A woman who became my *comadre* later always complained to me about her brother-in-law, a construction worker from northern Mexico. She was unhappy that he did not eat what the family offered him; he did not seem to like Yucatecan food in general and did not like to sleep in a hammock either. His wife's family felt that he refused their food because he disliked them, and this was creating tension in the family.

Eating their food, sleeping in a hammock, and participating in their daily activities helped narrow the cultural gap that existed at the beginning. Eventually I was offered *huipil* to wear, became a godparent for a couple of girls in the village, and began to be referred to as *comadre* within the chain of the extended families of my godchildren. Although I was physically different from the villagers, a Mestiza with short curly hair, emotionally they made me feel one of them. Some women even expressed their wish to have a child with my hair, but blue eyes. I also volunteered to take pictures of baptisims, as well as other special occasions such as weddings, for different families free of charge and so I became the village photographer for a year as well as a student of Mayan culture.

Entrance to the Community and Establishing a Network in Stira

After visits to northern and central Greece, Crete, and several villages on smaller islands, the village of Stira on the island of Evia (Euboea) was selected as the research site. It was chosen for the following reasons: First, the village is a typical rural Greek village. In addition, it had very little emigration compared to most villages its size. Most Greek villages have been abandoned by young people and now are inhabited mainly by people aged 60 years and older. Unlike most villages, Stira still has some young residents. Stira is also still an agricultural village, and the people continue to use traditional farming methods, plowing with horses and mules. The other major factor for selecting Stira for this research was that the community councilman and the priest, both highly respected, were willing to help. Furthermore, Stira is situated between two other small villages which are easily accessible: Kapsala, two kilometers (about 1.2 miles) east of Stira, and Reouzi, three kilometers (about 1.8 miles) west. These villagers have the same lifestyle and were useful in securing more women for the formal sample.

In Greek peasant culture, a woman is considered a threat to others just by the virtue of being a female unless she is under the control of a man; thus finding a defined role for a single woman who was a total stranger to the community was difficult.

On my first visit to Stira, some people thought that I was a tourist who had confused their village with some other tourist attractions on the island, such as Karistos, and tried to direct me back to the bus on which I arrived. However, because I spoke Greek and affirmed to them that Stira was where I wanted to be, they next thought I was a gypsy who had came to sell goods in the village. I had to do much explaining to convince them that I was not a gypsy. The priest and the councilman of the village were pleased that I chose Stira for the study and took great interest in easing my entrance into the community. I was introduced to the people as a writer who wanted to study the Greek rural culture.

After I decided on the village, finding housing became a problem because no extra houses were for rent at the moment. The villagers who had extra rooms in their households were reluctant to take in a stranger. In rural Greece, foreign women, especially Western Europeans and Americans, are characterized as being immodest and too outgoing, contrary to the villagers' moral code for women. Thus, women did not want to rent me a room in their households, fearing that I would disgrace their families. Finally, one family (a relative of my contact person in Greece) decided to rent me their son's room for the winter. Unlike people in Chichimila, the Greeks are very private people and are careful that family matters stay within the household; thus, occasionally, I was reminded not to mention to others what went on in the family. When winter ended, I was able to rent my own small place.

The first Sunday after I settled in, I went to church, because almost every woman in the village attends the Sunday liturgy. After the service, the priest spoke to the people about my work and stated that the people of Stira should be proud that I had chosen their village out of all those in Greece. He asked the women to cooperate with me. In addition, he told them that I was an Ethiopian, stating that the Greeks and Ethiopians have been friends for centuries. He emphasized the two cultures belong to the same Christian faith, and the people of Stira should make me feel welcome.

In addition to going to church, the councilman introduced me to his wife, a leading woman in the village. I became good friends with her and she, in turn, introduced me to a few other local women. By meeting one woman through another, I gradually expanded my network of women in the village. Because I was aware of the proper dress and moral codes, I was very careful of the way I dressed, what I did, and to whom I spoke. For example, I did not wear pants all through winter; although some girls in the village wear pants, the villagers were not pleased with such outfits, nor did they approve of heavy use of cosmetics.

Stira is a community where family secrecy and solidarity are strong. Women do not visit each other's houses casually, and they do not invite each other for meals, except for special occasions such as name days or weddings. People were polite and kind to me when I went to visit them. However, I did not have the open invitations I received in Chichimila, which is typical of some rural people in Greece. For example, the rural doctor was very much liked by the villagers, but in his four-year stay, not one family had invited him for a meal. Originally, my plan was to teach their children English free of charge, thereby establishing a role of being a teacher as well as someone who wanted to study their culture. In addition, this role would have given me another opportunity to meet with the mothers through the children. Unfortunately, I found out that one of the schoolteacher's wives, who had lived in the United States for a year, was teaching a few young children in the evening for a fee, and I had to abandon the idea of teaching because jeopardizing her income would have been inappropriate. Instead, I decided to approach the women for apprenticeship as I did in Chichimila. Thus, during the cold winter, I began knitting and needlework and started approaching women who would teach me certain local methods and designs of knitting. Because I already knew how to knit, I was able to exchange my designs with theirs. In a short time, the fact that I could knit and had an interest in learning more skills from them spread among the women. Because the people, men and women alike, have less work in winter and women have more time to engage in crafts, some women were able to teach me different ways of knitting, as well as cooking some Greek dishes and making confections. At times, some older women invited me to spend the afternoon with them, which allowed me to learn about the way they were raised, comparing the past to the present.

Even though it took time, the people of Stira finally accepted me in their community. With the exception of three households (one of the households that refused to be interviewed thought I was proselytizing for the Jehovah's Witnesses and the other two gave no reason), the villagers welcomed me when I went to their houses to interview them. In addition to being served sweets and preserves at every house, which is a rural Greek tradition, I was given gifts of hunks of feta cheese, loaves of homemade bread, and eggs. As a result, I never had to buy cheese or eggs after the first few weeks of my stay in the village.

6

Being a Woman in Chichimila

In the hierarchy of authority in the Yucatec Mayan culture, men are above women and the old above the young. A woman's activities center around the hearth, and women are not concerned with civic affairs (Redfield, 1941). Redfield's observation, made more than 40 years earlier, still holds true in Chichimila. In the Mayan culture, the formal acknowledgment of the different sex roles is the *hetzmek* ceremony, which is performed to ensure that an infant will develop properly. In Chichimila, this ceremony takes place three months after birth for boys and four months after birth for girls. During this ceremony, the godparent, a man for a boy and a woman for a girl, places in the child's hands those articles that the child will use in adult life. A female child is given tortillas, needles, thread, and kitchen utensils so that she will acquire the necessary skills to be a woman. She is also given a pencil and paper so that she will become literate, a modern addition to the ceremony because both boys and girls now go to school. A boy is given male items, such as a machete and a shotgun.

By age six or seven, the sex roles become more sharply differentiated. As soon as a girl turns seven, she begins to participate in the daily activities of women: She helps her mother take the *nixtamal* (corn for tortillas) to the corn mill and learns how to make tortillas. Gradually, she assumes a major role in preparing meals for the family and in other aspects of housework. A nine- to ten-year-old girl is a great help to her mother. In addition to sharing the housework responsibilities and taking care of younger siblings, she is also able to design and embroider her own *huipil.*

Figure 3. Four Generations of Mayan Women

Figure 4. A Mayan Woman Weaving a Henequen Bag

Figure 5. Two Young Mayans Dancing "Jarana," Mayan Folk Dance

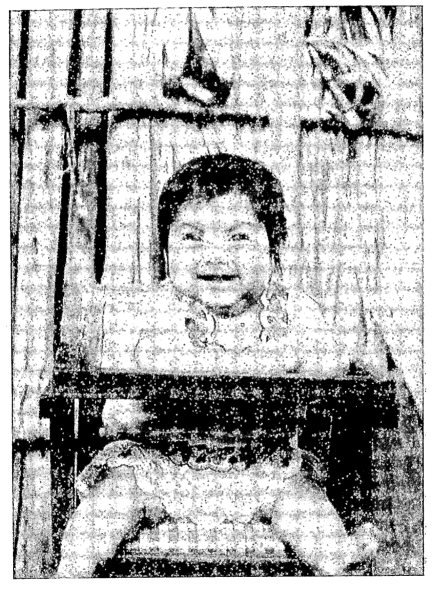

Figure 6. A Mayan Baby Girl

Figure 7. The Anthropologist with Two of Her Mayan Friends in Chichimila

Figure 8. Mayan Women Waiting to Vote for the 1981 Village Mayor

By age thirteen, most girls are capable of producing *huipiles* and hammocks for sale to supplement the family income. A young girl of 13 is taken out of school and stays home, refining her embroidery and hammock weaving skills until she is married, usually two or three years later. Even though a boy of eight or nine accompanies his father to the *milpa* and runs errands, his activities are not as structured as a girl's of his age. A boy has more time to play with other boys of his age, while girls are occupied by helping their mothers.

Thus, a woman in Chichimila learns the importance of her roles in the household and assumes responsibilities at an early age. She is brought up to be shy and soft-spoken; usually, she does not participate in conversations in the presence of males outside her family. Although a man's opinions carry greater weight than his wife's with regard to domestic matters, both husband and wife have a say on issues concerning the family's well-being , including the expenditure of money. With regard to childrearing decisions, however, the husband's mother, whether she lives in the same *solar* or not, always has more power in the decisionmaking. As older woman of the family, in many cases the husband's mother, is the one who gives the first diagnosis of a child's illness and provides a cure. A woman's path to higher social status is through her sons and grandsons. Once her sons are married, her daughters-in-law as well as her unmarried daughters are under her control. Once she acquires these resources, she has less to do in the house and her activities now revolve around taking care of her grandchildren and attending Mass. However, when all the family members are home for a meal, the senior woman in the household still cooks the tortillas. The rest of the female members of the family prepare the stew and pat the *masa*, the moist ground corn, into tortillas and hand it to her to put it on the metal grill to cook. The hearth is hers until she is incapable of performing this task.

The mother-and-son relationship is strong even after the son marries. If a son disobeys his mother, it creates a tremendous emotional crisis. For example, Doña Felipa in Chichimila has several sons and daughters. The father of the children died years ago, and she had to work hard to bring up her children. Of all her sons, Carlos, the youngest, was very helpful and often gave her money until he married. Doña Felipa did not want her son to marry Carmen, a Chichimila girl, but he disobeyed her and went ahead with the wedding. Doña Felipa was furious and refused to make the arrangements for the wedding feast. The wedding ceremony was held at the bride's house, and Carlos moved out of his mother's house. Afterward, Doña Felipa began to feel sick and lost weight.

Gradually, her illness became severe. All of her children, including Carlos, tried to find a cure for her illness and took her to both traditional and modern specialists. Her condition did not improve, however. The villagers felt that she had become sick because Carlos had broken her heart and caused a nervous ailment (*nerviosidad*). Everyone feared that she would die.

The mother-and-son tie is glorified. The woman is the one who suffers for her children while they are growing up. Mothers are known to use their children's love and sentiments to make their children feel guilty when they disobey. When a difference of opinion exists between the wishes of one's wife and those of one's mother, a man is expected to choose his mother over his wife. The villagers believe that there are always plenty of women for possible mates but there is only one mother.

Women's Daily Activities

The first thing a woman does when she gets out of her hammock is to light her cooking fire and prepare her husband's *pozole*, a drink made from corn. The wife usually gets up before 5:00 a.m. to prepare the *pozole* because the male adults in her household leave for the field very early in the morning, before the sun gets too hot. The corn is cooked and ground fresh that morning. Her husband and sons take this moist ground corn and water with them to the *milpa* where, around noon, they mix the corn and water for their lunches.

Corn is the staple food, eaten mostly as tortillas. The grains are soaked in lime water overnight to loosen the husk and then boiled until somewhat soft. Then the husk is removed and the *nixtamal*, the kernels, are ground into a paste called *masa*, at one of the two mills in the village. When the *masa* is ready, the Mayan woman pats out tortillas and cooks them on a *comal*, an iron griddle. The patting is done on a piece of plastic placed on a small round stool. The woman puts a small quantity of the *masa* on the piece of the plastic and pats it with the palm of the hand into a thin, round pancake. This is cooked on the hot griddle for a few minutes, turned over, and then removed from the griddle and put over hot coals from the hearth for a few more minutes. This process puffs the tortilla and as soon as it starts puffing, the woman removes it from the coals and pats in on the round stool. After the air is out, the tortilla is put in a round gourd to keep it warm until all the *masa* is cooked.

The basis for every meal is *masa*. Some of the most common variations are *chachakua*, made by rolling small pieces of chicken, a slice of egg, and a slice of tomato into a thick patted *masa* and wrapping it in a banana leaf, then steaming it. This is usually prepared for special occasions. Other important maize products are *pazole, atole,* and *pinole. Pozole* is a ball of *masa* taken by the men to the *milpa.* A small piece of *masa* is broken off and added to water in a *jicara* and the mixture is drunk. *Atole* is a hot gruel made from *masa.* The pieces of *masa* are broken and added to water and boiled for half an hour or so until the mixture thickens. It is drunk with sugar or hot pepper. *Atole* is also given to young children and sick people. It is prepared in almost every household in October and November when the new harvest of fresh maize is in. During this time, people invite each other for a *jicara* of *atole* and boiled corn on the cob, called *pib. Pinole* is ground, burnt corn used as a coffee drink. Tortillas are eaten at every meal. Black beans, usually boiled with some herbs such as *apazote,* or ground into thick puree are another important element of the diet. At times, the diet includes some yellow squash, squash seeds, onions, tomatoes, and hot chili peppers. The only green vegetable that is eaten is *chaya,* the leaf of a green bushy plant found in most of the *solares.* The leaves are boiled and eaten plain or stuffed in *tamales,* a steamed *masa.* Fresh mint is also used in scrambled eggs.

Although most people own one or two pigs and a few chickens, these animals are raised for cash. Most villagers' diets rarely contain meat, eggs, milk, or green vegetables. Occasionally, a family may have a couple of eggs, but meat is eaten very rarely, only on festive occasions. Food sharing is very common with kin and *compadres,* godparents, especially when one has prepared a special dish with meat. Milk is very expensive and must be bought from Valladolid or Can Cun, in the form of imported powdered milk. Only a very few people could afford to buy milk; it is bought mainly for babies and usually mixed with *atole,* the corn gruel. Overall, their diets are protein deficient.

While the men of the house are away, the woman prepares *nix-tamal,* the corn for tortillas. In the morning, the woman rinses the corn that had been left to soak overnight and gets it ready to be taken to the mill. By then the children are up and she prepares breakfast for them. If the family has money, the breakfast will consist of hot cocoa without milk and *pan frances* (a store-bought white bread). Otherwise, she prepares some *atole* and coffee for herself; if she does not have instant coffee, she makes a drink of *pinole.*

After breakfast, she washes the dishes, straightens the house, folds the hammocks and hangs them on the walls, sweeps the floor, fills her water containers from the nearest well, and feeds the animals. Then, she puts a pot of water and black beans to boil on the cooking fire. Once in a while she may cook something different, but most households eat beans every day. While the beans are cooking on a low fire, she goes to the mill to get her *nixtamal* ground.

A woman socializes and catches up with the latest gossip in the village at the mill while waiting for her turn. When she returns to her house, she does her wash until noon. Most households wash clothes frequently and the ones with small babies wash every day. About noon, she starts to make tortillas. Her children (and her husband, if he has not gone to the *milpa*), eat hot tortillas and bean soup while she continues making tortillas, until the *masa* (corn dough) is finished. She usually eats last.

Afternoons are less demanding. Some women take naps, others embroider or make strings from henequen fiber, and some weave hammocks. In the late afternoon, women bathe themselves and their young children and put on clean clothes. About 6:00 p.m., most women, especially older women, go to Mass. Because the main meal is eaten at noon, women usually do not have to prepare dinner. Dinner consists of hot cocoa and some bread or tortillas left over from lunch. Occasionally, a woman makes *panuchos*, fried tortilla and beans for dinner.

In addition to domestic activities, most women go to the field with their husbands and help there. Between the corn plants, they grow tomatoes, squash, radishes, chile, and *cilantro*, a green herb much like coriander. Women sell tomatoes, radishes, and chile peppers in the market in Valladolid. They also sell hammocks and *huipiles* made by themselves or a female member of the household. When teenage daughters and daughters-in-law are living with her, a woman has more time to do things other than the routine housework. Often, this time is used for going to Mass every day and visiting friends. Although women generally do the family cooking, it is not uncommon for men to help in preparing food for a wife who is ill and has no other helper.

The above description of roles applies to most women in Chichimila. However, a few village women have slightly different activities from their daily cooking and housework. For example, a woman whose husband is a merchant takes on responsibilities in the shop as well as at home. Doña Lupita, the wife of a merchant and mother of eight children, spends equal time at home and in the shop helping her husband. When her husband was drunk and out for a week, Doña Lupita had to tend the shop full-time.

A divorced woman sometimes has to take care of her children alone. Three of the women in my study sample were abondoned by their husbands. Marriages in Chichimila are either common-law unions or performed by religious authorities, but no one goes through the process of a legal divorce in Chichimila. It is not unusual for a man to simply abandon his wife and children and live with another woman in another village. Abandoned women support themselves and their families by taking odd jobs in the village or outside in some other villages. There were no prostitutes in the village, but men are accustomed to having secret lovers, and divorced women are sometimes suspected of supporting their families in this way.

If a woman never marries, she remains the responsibility of her father and brothers. There are a few middle-aged women in the village who never married and live with their brothers. Most of the women who remain unmarried do so due to illness. The unmarried woman shares responsibilities in the house with her sisters-in-law, but has more time than most women her age for weaving hammocks and embroidering. She never gains adult status and is addressed throughout her life with no formal respect and is always called by her first name. A 54-year-old woman in the village was referred to as *muchacha*, a term used for a little girl. In the Mayan culture, the status of adulthood is not based on chronology alone. One has to be married, have children, and proceed through the socially defined roles in the culture in order to become an adult. The status of an unmarried woman in the Maya culture is static, locked in the category of childhood.

The situation of women healers, particularly midwives, is also distinctive. Much of the midwife's time is spent away from home, and there are times during labor, when she must stay overnight at her clients' homes. Because all the midwives in Chichimila are older than 60 years old, they have daughters-in-law to do their household duties.

One woman in the village whose position is unique is the health promoter, Doña Maria. In addition to her role as a health promoter, she is the postal agent for the village and gets the mail for Chichimila twice a week from Valladolid and distributes it from her house. She is also active in village politics and was a councilwoman (*regidora*) for the village *presidente* at the time of my fieldwork. Moreover, whenever a dance or a fiesta such as a *corrida* (bullfight) is held, she checks tickets at the entrance and is paid 100 pesos ($4.00 U. S. in 1981) each night. At the same time, she is responsible for her household's cooking and washing.

Doña Maria's husband left her 18 years ago for a woman living in another village. She has raised her five children alone; two sons were still living with her at the time of my fieldwork. She also cares for her 80-year-old mother and helps her financially. Doña Maria has an advantage over other women in the village in being literate in Spanish, and she has pursued a role different from that which her culture has designated for women.

Mayan women are overtly quiet and patient people. Physical fights between women are unknown. Bad feelings arising between neighbors are usually caused by disputes over animals. For example, women often find it difficult to convincingly identify those of their fowls that are wandering into a neighbor's *solar*, and the neighbor may mistakenly claim a turkey or a chicken that does not belong to her. Or it sometimes happens that a woman's hen lays eggs in somebody else's *solar*, and these are claimed by the owner of the *solar*. Some owners tie a bright piece of cloth or thread on the leg of their birds to prevent them from getting mixed up with other people's poultry. Sometimes such disputes are settled by the village *presidente*. Village men are also generally peaceful and friendly. When violence does occur, it is most often preceded by consumption of alcohol.

In Chichimila, drunkenness is frequent among men, particularly young men. Most families have a father, a son, or both who drink often. In addition to consuming the family's modest resources, these men sometimes become belligerent and abuse their wives and children. The village has several *cantinas*, and men do not have to go outside the village to get drink. On Saturday and Sunday, when the men working in Can Cun come home for the weekend, it is very rare to find a sober man in the village. This is typical of the villages around Valladolid. Drunks fight in the street, usually with family members who try to take them home. Those driving through the villages on Saturday or Sunday afternoon must be very careful because the streets are occupied by staggering drunks trying to make it home. Some men get drunk during weekdays and skip work.

In Chichimila, the major sources of stress in a woman's life are her husband's and sons' drinking habits, money, work load, pregnancy, children's health, and her mother-in-law.

Women are concerned about their husbands' and sons' drinking, but they feel powerless to change the situation. In Chichimila, a wife does not have any authority over her husband's behavior. It is expected that a woman will not scold her husband for drinking. I was told that the only person who has authority over a man is his mother. If he will not listen to her, it is certain he will not listen to his wife. Some women worry every weekend whether their husbands and sons will come home safe without having a fight with another drunk. Doña Juanita, whose husband gets drunk every weekend, said that she sometimes sends her younger son to look after his father when she suspects that he is out drinking. If the boy reports that his father is becoming belligerent, she goes out to bring him home. Doña Juanita is 37 years old with seven children. Her husband is 44 years old and owns a *cantina* in addition to a plot of land for his *milpa*. I have seen bruises on her arms from struggling to bring him home so that he will not become involved in fights. Another woman said that she once had a miscarriage because her husband was drunk and pushed her down when she was seven months pregnant. Widowed or divorced women seemed the most distressed about their sons' drinking habits: After all the years they suffered to raise their children, they are heartbroken to see their sons waste their money and ruin their health.

Alcoholism, I was told, is a new phenomenon in the villages. Some older women said that their men drank occasionally at local fiestas but never had the money to go out and get drunk every week. Some feel that the drinking habits of their men are due to working in Can Cun and having money in hand. Men drink in a group; rarely does a man drink alone.

Two women with whom I became good friends often cried over their drunken sons. Both of these women are heads of their households (one is a widow and the other is a divorcee). Jose, the son of the widow, is 20 years old, and Felipe, the son of the divorcee, is 19. Both completed elementary school and each had a year of junior high school. These boys started to drink when they were 15 years old, and now they continued to drink with friends of the same age. A couple of times when their sons came home drunk, the mothers called the village *comisario* (deputy) and had them hauled to jail for 24 hours in the village *palacio municipal* (town hall). However, it seemed to have no effect on them. In 1980, Jose and Felipe went to Can Cun for the first time and found jobs as busboys. A dozen cans of beer costs 216 pesos (approximately $8.00 U. S. in 1981). In 1981 the average daily wage for those who worked in Can Cun was 170 pesos ($6.80 U. S.), and Jose said that he drinks at least 20 cans of beer at a time, once or twice a week. It was their first time away from home and both boys found it very difficult to adjust to city life. After a few months, they were both fired and returned home. The summer of the same year, they got temporary jobs with the Census Bureau taking a village census. Again, they nearly lost their jobs because of drinking.

These two boys are typical of the young men of their age in Chichimila, unable to commit themselves to a permanent job, unable to locate themselves in either the past or the present. They feel that they are above the traditional way of life, because they have been to school, know how to read and write, and are ambitious for a better standard of living than their parents have. However, they lack the skills or the means to fit into the modern world. They apparently do not know what they want, and they are not motivated to pursue either a modern or traditional lifestyle. They just "hang around" with their friends, who are in the same situation. Whenever one of them gets money, they get together and drink. When they are sober, they all talk about getting jobs, going to Can Cun or Cozumel to look for employment. Some of their friends who did not finish elementary school, were willing to work in construction in Can Cun, but Jose and Felipe felt they should have better opportunities because they had additional schooling. I had several talks with these boys, and it was clear that they knew the sorts of problems to which alcohol can lead. They said that they drink to have a good time, *por gusto*; their friends invite them to drink, they take turns buying rounds, and, before they know it, they are drunk.

Both boys eventually decided to try the *milpa*. Because their mothers are poor, have no land, and do not belong to the *ejido* system, the sons rented a plot of land, cleared it, and prepared a *milpa* for the first time in their lives. Their mothers were excited and very supportive. Jose and Felipe had cleared a large area of land, and all work had been done by hand in the heat of the day. They invited me along with their mothers to watch them burn their field. This seems to have been a turning point in the lives for Felipe and Jose. There are many other marginal young people in Chichimila and many other mothers who worry about their children's future and their own existence, because parents depend on their sons' support in their old age.

For the typical Mayan woman, money is a constant worry. The source of her worries is the fact that her husband wastes the family's budget on alcohol. The money from selling corn from the harvest is usually in the husband's hands, and unless he is strongly self-disciplined, most of it is used on beer and *aguardiente* (local rum). Thus, the woman has to find other sources of money in order to support her children. Most women grow tomatoes, squash, radishes, and some herbs and make *tamales* and other food to sell in the market in Valladolid. The majority of the women are also involved in some type of handicraft, making hammocks and embroidery for sale. Older women are usually engaged in making strings from henequen fibers which they sell to others who make *saboucan* (henequen bags), and hammocks, etc. Doña Felice, who is 80 years old, still makes such string and her daughter sells it for her. Before the introduction of machine-made cotton thread, the Mayans made hammocks from henequen fiber. Chichimila is one of the few villages where they still make henequen hammocks.

Pregnancy is also something that the women worry about. Even though fecundity has high cultural value for the Maya, the physical stress of constant childbearing is great. Unless she is sterile, a married woman in Chichimila is either pregnant or lactating throughout most of her reproductive life. Some Mayan men are helpful and fetch water or look after the children as their wives approach delivery. But usually women assume their normal work load up to the last day of their pregnancies. Besides the physical stress, pregnancy also induces anxiety because it is regarded as being an unpredictable and dangerous state. The Mayan women, particularly young married women, are ready to accept family planning programs, but men want more children. Even if they have several children, men feel that they will lose control over the sexual activities of their wives if the women are on birth control programs. Thus, men do not approve of their wives using any birth control methods. One woman in the study said that after her eighth childbirth she arranged with a doctor in Valladolid to have her tubes tied without telling her husband.

Women are physically stressed by their heavy work loads. They complained of persistent shoulder and neck muscle aches. Moreover, women are worried about the health of their children and their well-being. A mother-in-law could also add to one's hardship if she is too authoritarian and unwilling to help in the household tasks. When I first explained to the women of Chichimila that I was interested in learning about the lifestyle of Mayan women, most adult women stated that life for Mayan women is very difficult and the daily worries are numerous. My own observation of these women's daily existence reaffirms their statement and indeed, life is difficult for Mayan women.

7

Being a Woman in Stira

In Greek culture, an individual's role at any one moment depends very much on the person's sex, age, and status. According to the traditional Greek symbolic classification of sexes, men and women form a complementary opposition according to which men have a natural association with the sacred world and a closer derivation from God, while women are associated with the world of the demons. This basic characterization of men and women is based on the creation story of Adam and Eve and the Fall. Thus, women in Greek society are considered inferior to men, seductive, stupid, and fearful, endangering their houses by their sexual weakness and their irresponsibility in the matter of gossip. Moreover, the sexual nature of women is judged as intrinsically impure, and menstruation is seen as evidence of this impurity (Campbell, 1964; du Boulay, 1974; Friedle, 1962).

This is an unchanging classificaton and regardless how important the feminine role in the Greek society, the status of men's superiority and women's inferiority remains constant. In Greek culture, one of the most important qualities a woman can have is a sense of shame. She should be aware of the significance of honorable and dishonorable actions, and she should prefer always the honorable actions. The Greek word *dropi* (shame) implies a sense of sexual modesty, a quality that women especially possess by nature, the one quality that redeems them from domination by their destructive sexual attributes. A woman's promiscuity is seen by Greek society as the gravest possible threat because it destroys the existence of the family. Therefore, an unchaste woman

Figure 9. Three Generations of Greek Women

Figure 10. A Greek Woman Returning from Milking Her Goats

Figure 11. A Greek Woman Spinning Wool

Figure 12. A Greek Woman Crocheting for Her Granddaughter's Dowry

Figure 13. A Greek Woman Taking Hay to Her Livestock

Figure 14. The Village "Agora" (Center)

is incapable of being a wife or a mother. Generally, girls are considered a potential danger to the family's honor because of their sensuality and the fear that they may bring shame to the family's honor. They are also a liability to their families because of the economic burden of their dowries they need in order to get married. Thus, families prefer to have many sons and only one daughter. Rural people especially feel resentful when they have more than one daughter. In Stira, a woman told me that when her daughter-in-law gave birth to three girls and no sons, her husband was so angry that when she returned from the hospital he locked the door of his house and would not let her in. Girls are believed to bring poverty and stress to their families.

In rural Greece, a girl starts to help her mother at home at age seven, preparing food and doing errands. She is restricted from playing outside her own house, while a boy of the same age is free to play ball with his friends. The girl learns from an early age the sense of shame and modesty. The villagers want to emphasize in their children an inner sense of embarrassment at the thought of improperly revealing oneself, either the physical self (modesty) or the inner emotional self (Friedle, 1962). Both a man and a woman are expected to be modest and keep the family's honor. However, if a man is dishonorable it is thought to be because of a situation against his control in which he was tempted beyond a reasonable level.

A girl of ten is taught to embroider, crochet, and knit and prepare mantel pieces and tablecloths for her dowry. Traditionally, both boys and girls are required to help at home and in the fields starting at an early age. However, children now must attend school, and they have little time to help in the fields. The girls still help their mothers after school. Even though both boys and girls finish primary school, girls are discouraged from continuing their education beyond junior high school, because obtaining a high school diploma requires that they go to Athens or other cities. In addition, education is not considered important for a girl and sending her to a city is increasing the chance that she will jeopardize the family's honor. Instead, she is kept home to work on her dowry and help her mother until an appropriate match is found for her.

Unlike the boys, the girls in Stira and other rural areas of Greece are caught between rural, traditional values and modern, urban values. For example, Panagicha is 22 years old and was able to finish high school in Halkida by staying with relatives. Unlike her older sister who remained home after junior high school and waited to get married, Panagicha wanted to receive a higher education. Thus, she sat for the Greek university entrance examination and passed for one of the schools. However, her father refused to allow her to attend the college that is approximately a six-hour drive from the village. Because her father did not have a son, he was willing to let her finish high school, but he could not tolerate her seeking a college education. Panagicha had been out of high school for four years and she was staying home hoping that some one would come along to marry her. Because an appropriate match is unlikely to be found in the village, she will probably marry a city man.

The urban culture is showing its impact in the rural areas of Greece. Young girls' dress styles in Stira are similar to those in Athens, and the villages seem to be tolerant of their daughters wearing pants, which was unthinkable a few years earlier. However, a girl's ambition for educa-tion is still not acceptable in Stira.

In Greek society, the only way a woman gains status and becomes redeemed from all her natural negative traits is by being a wife and mother, under the protection of a man (Hirschon, 1978). Once a woman is mar-ried, she becomes the pillar of the house; she represents in herself the history and continuity of the family. Thus, the status of a woman who faithfully observes her roles as a wife and mother differs from the negative traits attributed to women. A married woman is the moral solidarity of her household. In village cultural values, physical strength and robustness, rather than fragile beauty, are the physical characteristics admired in a wife and a mother. Women work hard both in the house and in the field. Most older women in the village married in their late twenties or early thirties. It was explained to me that in those days a family wanted their son to get married to a strong and hard-working woman to contribute to the family's labor force.

In Greek culture, a woman is freed from male dominance only through her sons. Male children are valued because they carry the family's name. A woman takes her husband's family name; couples with no son adopt a boy so that one's family is not ended. Women with no children are considered unfortunate; thus, women without children visit different healers and shrines in the hopes of conceiving.

In Greek culture, a strong attachment exists between a son and his mother, and the status of a mother with married sons is considerable in the extended family. She embodies the integrity and solidarity of her family. A mother is believed to have sacrificed herself for her children; she was the one who spent more time with the children when they were young. A father is usually the disciplinary figure in the family and spends most of his time outside of the house working in the field or visiting with his friends and playing cards in the coffeehouse. In return for her unconditional love and care, a mother is respected by her sons and she has an absolute right to be the head of the extended family households of her married sons. As a woman ages, particularly in her postmenopausal years, she gains a new freedom from the authority of her husband and from the restrictions of social convention. She is no longer considered a threat to the community at an older age, especially if her husband is dead, because she no longer is considered sensual.

In rural Greek communities, the unmarried woman and widow are treated as underprivileged members of the society. Particularly, a young widow is considered disruptive to the village moral standards (du Baulay, 1974; Hirschon, 1978). Because she is known to be awakened to a sensuality that is neither controlled nor satisfied by a man, she is expected to have a high degree of sense of shame and modesty. She should not talk to any man outside of her kin nor visit neighbors on name day celebrations, because she is desired by all, though available to none. She is looked upon as a source of conflict between unrelated men and women. Every action of a widow is watched by the villagers and is interpreted as an effort to look for a man. A widow is prone to gossip and mockery until she gets old. In Stira, as well as in other rural areas of Greece, mockery and gossip are most effective agents of social control.

Women's Daily Activities

Regardless of the season, the woman of a household is the first to rise in the morning, usually at 5:00 a.m. In winter, the animals are kept close by the house; thus, her first job is to take care of the animals. The work of feeding the animals and cleaning the pen is shared both by the husband and wife. After taking care of the animals, then the wife comes home and prepares coffee and *trahana* for breakfast. Beginning in the spring until fall, the animals are kept away from the house, usually in a different location from the family's farm, up on a hill. Only the donkeys, mules, and horses are still kept near because they are used to ride to the field and carry loads. A dog usually guards the goats and the sheep. During these seasons, a woman must prepare her husband's lunch, which he takes with him to the field; this usually consists of a big piece of homemade bread, feta cheese, olives, tomatoes, and a little bottle of homemade resinated white wine. While the husband goes to the field, the woman loads big cans of water for the animals and her milk containers on a mule or a donkey and heads to where the animals are kept.

During the milking season, the woman has to process the goats' and sheep's milk into cheese immediately. Generally, she milks the animals twice each day. Milking is not only a woman's job; a husband also milks when his wife has other priorities.

Cooking, washing, and caring for the children are a woman's job. A man who participates in such culturally defined categories of woman's roles is looked down upon by others and is a bad reflection on his wife. Apparently, the women do not want men involved in housework because the house is the domain of the woman. Thus, any woman who allows her husband to do cleaning and washing is subject to mockery and gossip. However, a man may help in the house if his wife is sick and does not have anyone else to help her.

Wheat is the main staple food. The family uses its own wheat to make bread, which is the basic food of the people. Wheat is also used to make noodles and a kind of cereal called *trahana*, which is similar to cracked wheat. In late August, people roast a few ears of fresh corn; otherwise, it is used for chicken feed. In Stira, a typical household's diet consists of bread, feta cheese, eggs, milk, legumes or a variety of vegetables, depending on the season of the year, and fruit. The most important vegetables in winter are the different kinds of wild greens called *horta* that grow at the hillsides and the fields. Collecting *horta* is a woman's job. Some of these wild greens are available throughout the year and some are seasonal. Besides *horta* and cabbage, the villagers do not have other vegetables in winter. The fruits cultivated in the village are eaten as they ripen. The women also prepare some sweet preserves called *glico kutaliou*, which are served when a guest comes to visit. Serving a spoonfull of sweet preserve with a glass of water or home made liquor is a standard form of village hospitality.

A woman also works in the fields most of the time and leaves the responsibility for housework to her teenage daughter if she has one. If not, she has to make the beds, sweep the floor and wash the dishes before she leaves for the field. When she and her husband come home, she prepares dinner while her husband washes, puts on clean clothes, and relaxes. After dinner, the husband usually goes to one of the coffeehouses in the village to visit with his friends, play cards, and have a cup of coffee or some locally made liquor called *tzipouro*.

One never sees a woman in Stira sitting idle. Between work, especially in winter and spring, a woman goes out to the near by hills and fields with a small knife and a bag to pick up variety of greens such as dandelions. The vegetable garden in her backyard is also her responsibility. She has to weed and water the garden daily. When she is done with her housework and farm duties, she knits, crochets a bed spread or mantel pieces, or embroiders. The women in Stira also spin the wool from their sheep and weave rugs, blankets, and sheets. Women do not visit their neighbors often and those who do are prone to be gossiped about for neglecting their work because women are assumed never to have time for leisure without neglecting their duties. If a woman must visit a sick neighbor or relative, she always takes with her knitting or crochet to attend to while visiting. The hostess also takes out her craft and both women work while visiting and drinking coffee. A woman is judged by others on how industrious she is. The honorable woman always avoids being seen in the agora conversing with men. Even when she goes to the stores, which are all in the agora, she usually takes the back road wherever there is one.

Although the sex roles are clearly defined, the family as a unit shares all the responsibilities in the household. Girls are especially helpful to their mothers and boys help in taking care of animals after school and running errands. A woman's activities in the field vary among seasons. In early fall, she is out picking olives. This is a tedious job requiring the help of all family members. Even grandma must help to accomplish the task before the cold winter arrives. A woman has more time to attend to her knitting and crocheting in winter because there is usually very little to do outside the house until early spring. In spring and summer, she spends more time working out in the field as well as at home.

In Stira, the activities of wives of those who are not involved in farming differ from the rest. However, because almost every one in the village owns some sheep and goats, the women are in charge of the animals even though they do no farm labor. The wives of those who own coffeehouses and small stores spend their time helping their husbands serving the customers in the stores. For example, Kiria Kula and her husband own a coffeehouse and her time is divided between her housework and the shop. She rises early and starts the meal for noon, cleans her house, washes the dishes, and makes the beds. She also prepares homemade sweets to sell in the shop, such as rice pudding and almond cookies. The shop is approximately a five-minute walk from her house, and she spends most of her time going back and forth from her house to the shop. Most of the time, she stays in the shop until 10:00 p.m. The coffeehouse is an all-male domain, and no one talks to her except when they want to order coffee or refreshments. She is constantly washing coffee cups and glasses. Still, she does some kind of crocheting or knitting in the shop between serving the customers.

A couple of village women do not have responsibilities outside of their houses. One such woman is Kiria Anna whose husband owns a large, prosperous, pig farm. The pigs are kept outside of the village and looking after pigs is mainly a man's job. Thus, Kiria Anna has more time to do embroidery and other crafts because she does not have to work in the field.

Generally, Greek rural women are muscular and hard-working. A woman may ride a mule or a donkey to go to the field and walk back, five to eight kilometers, loading the mule with hay and other feed for the goats and sheep. If a woman's husband is missing, she does the plowing. As a result of hard work in extreme weather, the women look older than their actual age; however, they are physically strong and healthy-looking.

One of the major causes of health problems for Greek women is *setnaxoria* (worry) about their children's well-being. Due to the emigration of the rural young to cities to find a future assumed to be better, mothers in Stira are in a constant state of worry. After finishing junior high school, most of the young boys in the village leave Stira for Halkida or Karistos on the island, or Athens, in order to get a high school diploma or training in some kind of trade school. Others take manual jobs in an urban area, which they feel is a lot better than their father's existence. Although education is free in Greece, ensuring adequate funds to pay for their children's board and room as well as school supplies is a cause for constant concern and a major economic burden.

For those who have daughters, the source of *stenaxoria* is finding an appropriate husband. Moreover, the size of the dowry is one of the major factors in determining the kind of husband the daughter gets. Therefore, parents have to save some money by sacrificing other needs. Once a girl reaches puberty, her family members and relatives are busy finding her an appropriate match. In the meantime, she is watched very closely to control where she goes and with whom she associates, in order to avoid possible sources of damage to her reputation and her family's honor. A daughter's inappropriate behavior is blamed on her mother and apparent lack of supervision.

Besides their daily heavy work load, the women in Stira are responsible for taking care of their aged, frail in-laws. In most households, the mother or the father of the husband resides with the family, and the responsibility of looking after the elderly is left totally to the daughter-in-law. Women also expressed their worry about their own aging and the fear of becoming frail. Because the young are abandoning the village, they fear no one will be left to look after them when they grow old.

Unlike Chichimila, Stira does not seem to have an alcohol problem. Men do drink a lot of wine, but staggering drunks on the streets are not seen. This could be because the men in the village usually drink homemade wine with big meals.

As with Mayan woman, the major sources of stress for rural Greek women are worries about the well being of their children, economic hardship and taking care of frail elderly parents or in-laws. Overall, women in Stira describe the rural lifestyle as very tiring.

8

Comparing Reproductive Histories, Part I: From Menarche Through Childbearing

In order to explain the meaning and significance of menopause, the cultural interpretation of all reproductive phenomena, particularly menstruation, pregnancy, and the importance of fecundity must be understood. Based upon data derived from the unstructured and structured interviews, as well as the participant observation, the rest of the chapters provide an ethnography of the reproductive cycle, including menopause and its significance among Mayan and Greek women.

Menarche

Menarche represents an important developmental stage in a woman's life. Age at menarche has been of great interest to researchers because it demonstrates the difference in growth and development among children in industrialized and in some developing countries. Menarche is preceded by the appearance of the secondary sex characteristics and body changes that occur sometime between the ages of nine and 16: the breasts develop, body hair increases, body weight increases, a growth spurt occurs, skin glands become more active, and a change in body proportions takes place with the hips becoming fuller. Pubertal development may be fast or slow. On the average, menarche occurs between ages 12.8 and 13.2 years worldwide (Eveleth and Tanner, 1976). Environmental factors such as nutrition, socioeconomic status, altitude, and stress (environmental and emotional), as well as genetic heritage, and chronic illness have been proposed as factors affecting the age of menarche.

Moreover, significant hormonal changes occur at puberty. The gonadal, adrenal, and hypothalamic-hypophyseal hormones are of major importance and the interrelationship of these hormones controls the female reproductive cycle (Tanner, 1978; Petersen and Taylor, 1980). Menarche occurs after a series of changes in hormone secretion and somatic growth. These processes are, in turn, influenced by environmental and genetic factors.

Mayan and Greek Women's Perception of Menstruation

Menstruation is not simply a physiological process; it is linked with psychological, social, and cultural variables. Their various interaction patterns determine the perception of menstruation and its significance, both symptomatological and behavioral (Snowden and Christian, 1983). In some cultures, menstrual blood symbolizes both danger and power (Douglas, 1966), and the danger and impurity connected with women's sexual processes are controlled by taboos and restrictions on certain activities.

Mayan Women's Perception of Menstruation

For the Mayan women in the study sample, the mean age at onset of menarche was 13.3 (SD 1.3) (see Table 3). Only five women could not remember their ages at onset of menarche. In the Mayan culture, there is no ritual associated with menarche, nor is menstruation and its significance explained to a young girl before the onset of the first menses. It is considered a sin to tell a girl about menstruation before her first period or to explain anything to her about sex before marriage. Thus, the mothers I interviewed had not instructed their daughters, nor had their mothers instructed them. Most of these women remembered their first menses as a traumatic event. Only 35 percent of the women in the study knew about menstruation before the onset. Of the rest, some thought that they were sick and immediately told their mothers, others thought they had hurt themselves playing, and still others tried to hide the evidence.

Seventy-five percent of the women reported that they have no discomfort or pain related to menstruation; the rest suffered from stomach pains and backache. Among those who reported pain or discomfort, 50 percent claim to do nothing to relieve the pain. The rest used remedies purchased from either a local healer or local store.

At the onset of menarche in the Mayan culture, a young girl begins to observe the taboos associated with menstruating women. Among the Mayans, a menstruating woman is believed to carry an evil wind and is a danger to others, especially to a newborn baby.

In Chichimila, it is believed that if a menstruating woman visits a newborn baby, the umbilical cord of the baby will start to bleed and could cause death. Such a woman also should avoid passing by an area where men are digging wells because she can cause disasters such as cave-ins. Households with newborn babies hang *anona* leaves outside the door until the umbilical cord is dried off, to signal the villagers; men who are digging wells usually take the precaution of wearing a woman's garment (underwear, I was told) on their heads or hanging it on a stick nearby.

Women were very aware of their menstrual cycles, remembering onset of menarche, the number of menstruations between each pregnancy, and onset of menopause. What was more surprising was the awareness shown by Mayan men of their wives' menstrual cycles. The husbands who happened to be home at the time I conducted my interviews gave detailed accounts of the patterns and dates of their wives' menses. Husbands of menopausal women claimed to remember the time span between menses at the time their wives began having irregular periods; they also claimed to know the month of the last menses.

The women's understanding of menstrual blood is that it is dirty blood and needs to be changed every month. One physician in Valladolid told me that the Mayan women who came to him for treatment referred to their menstrual cycles as *la luna*, the moon. They used phrases such as, "I have not seen the moon this month," or "I still see the moon." The menstrual cycle is referred to as the moon because the moon and women's menstruation have 28-day cycles.

Among the women in Chichimila, the most serious problem for a young woman is *pasmo*, which is due to delayed menstruation or detained flow. Women fear that the retention of "dirty blood" can cause health problems. To avoid getting *pasmo*, a menstruating woman refrains from the consumption of cold drinks, bathing with cold water, wetting her feet, or walking in the rain. She also avoids drinks or foods with citrus ingredients, such as lemons or oranges, when her period is due.

It is believed that the cold drinks and citrus fruit thicken the blood and prevent it from flowing. One of my informants reported that she developed *pasmo* once because she was caught in the rain a day before she was expecting her period. Women stay home during their menses and arrange their activities around their menses. However, women distinguish *pasmo* from amenorrhea following childbirth and the cessation of the menses due to menopause. Mayans use oregano as a remedy for a young woman with the problem of *pasmo*, menstrual pain, or an irregular menstrual cycle. The herb is boiled and the tea is drunk in the morning on an empty stomach for several days. Concentrated oregano tea is believed to increase the menstrual flow. Women believe that it can also cause hemorrhaging, and so it is not given to a pregnant woman, for fear of causing miscarriage.

At age 13, or at actual onset of menarche, a girl is taken out of school. Those who are allowed to continue school miss classes for three or four days each month during the time of their menses. However, very few households allow their daughters to continue to go to school after menarche. Moreover, Mayan women wear white garments and are afraid of menstrual spotting or *mancha*. The only sanitary devices that the Mayan women use are rags, washed and kept ready for each time. Sanitary napkins are available in Valladolid, but village women cannot afford them.

Because menstruation is characterized by activity restrictions, food taboos, fear of spotting, the annoyance of washing rags, and the need to keep it secret from the young girls in the family, Mayan women welcome the cessation of the menstrual cycle during pregnancy.

Greek Women's Perception of Menstruation

For Greek women in the study, the mean age at onset of menarche was 14 (SD 1.9), with ages ranging between 11 and 18. Like the Mayan women, the Greeks also have taboos and restrictions related to menstruation and childbearing. Menstruating women, women who just gave birth, and a woman after miscarriage are all considered impure and polluted. A menstruating woman is not allowed to participate in religious activities for she is considered unclean. She should not go to church; should not even light the candle or touch the icons in her shrine at home; should not go where the family's wine is because it would become flat; she should not bake bread because the dough would not rise; she should not touch the feta cheese because it would become contaminated and turn yellow; she should also avoid touching the oil barrels because the oil is burned at church and in the small shrine at home.

The above taboos also apply to a woman who just gave birth. After a woman gives birth, she should stay at home for 40 days. She should not visit anybody until the 40 days are over, because it is believed that she would bring disaster to the family she visited. After 40 days, the village priest blesses the house, the mother, and the baby; they become free to move around again.

Menstrual blood is perceived to have uncontrollable power and should be prevented from contaminating anything related to the church such as oil, wine, and bread, substances used in the Greek Orthodox religion. As with the Mayans, a menstruating woman should not drink cold drinks, bathe with cold water, and should not eat oranges or lemons because cold substances and citrus fruit are believed to stop the menstrual flow. However, the young Greek women seem to disregard the above taboos, with the exception of church participation.

Rural Greeks also believe that informing their daughters before onset of menarche is a sin. Thus, 50 percent of the women in the study stated that they did not know what it was and were frightened at the time of their first menses. They believed that menstruation was a curse as a result of Eve's sin and that women had to suffer. Menstrual blood was considered bad blood and women should be rid of it. Thus, heavy menstrual flow was considerd good because it cleans the blood well. In addition, heavy flow meant more children. For Greek women, menstruating every month was a sign of good health. Thus, the longer one had her period the healthier she was. One woman mentioned that she knew an old woman who had her period until age 60. This woman was said to look healthy, walked like a young girl at an old age, and was very strong because she had her period for a long time and her blood was cleaned well. Like Mayan women, Greeks also used herbs and spices such as oregano, sage, and cinnamon, to treat menstrual pain and discomfort.

Table 3

Comparison of the Distribution of Age at Onset of Menarche For Mayan and Greek Women

	Mayan (N=102)		Greek (N=94)	
Age at Onset of Menarche	*N*	*Percent*	*N*	*Percent*
Early Onset				
11	4	3.9	8	8.5
12	27	26.5	20	21.3
Average Onset				
13	27	26.5	17	18.1
14	25	24.5	16	17.0
Late Onset				
15	15	14.7	14	14.9
16	3	2.9	7	7.4
17	1	1.0	10	10.6
18	0	0	2	2.1

The Importance of Fecundity and Pregnancy

Mayan Women

In Chichimila, once a woman is married, she is expected to bear a child within one or two years. In the cases where this does not happen, families worry that the woman may be sterile, a very unfortunate situation both for the woman and the family. Sterility is legitimate grounds for divorce. In cases where a woman proves to be sterile, it often happens that either she is abandoned by her husband or he develops a liaison with another woman who can bear children for him. The inability to have children is always assumed to be the woman's fault, and generally traced to *maldad* or *hechiceria* (sorcery) or *matris infantil*,(infant womb).

Flora, a 30-year-old woman, told me that because she could not bear a child she had consulted various healers including a physician in Valladolid. She said that the doctor told her that she has "infant womb": however, she felt that her sterility had been caused by her mother-in-law, who lives in another village. According to Flora, this woman, who had not wanted Flora to marry her son, had cast a spell, *hechiceria*, on her. Illnesses or unusual situations that do not respond to treatment are thought to be caused by sorcery. Flora's husband has had two children out of wedlock, with the approval of the members of his family.

Sonia, who is 25 years old and has been married for ten years, is also worried about losing her husband. According to Sonia's mother-in-law, Sonia's husband had been sympathetic and has not left her. He is a convert to an evangelical denomination, an *hermano*. Because his religion insists that a man have only one woman, his wife, he has no alternative. This lack of an alternative worries his mother.

Women are afraid to use oral contraceptives for fear of becoming sterile. Luisa, age 22, was married at age 18. Her husband works in Can Cun and comes home only on weekends. She has been unable to conceive for two years. Worried by this situation, Luisa's mother-in-law took her to the *h-men* to be blessed and treated with herbs; she also took Luisa to physicians in Valladolid. Finally, a physician in Valladolid suggested that Luisa move to Can Cun and live with her husband, instead of seeing him only on weekends. A few months after moving to Can Cun, Luisa became pregnant. Subsequently, she returned to Chichimila, finished her pregnancy, and gave birth to a baby girl. Unlike her friends, Luisa did not want to have another child right away. She claims that she wants to join a family planning program, but her husband, her mother, and mother-in-law are strongly opposed to this. They believe that because she had a problem conceiving, she would never be able to have another child if she started taking contraceptives. Her husband had forbidden her to be friends with the health promoter because he believes that this woman wants to recruit young women for the family planning program provided by the Mexican government.

As noted by some social scientists, parents in peasant societies consciously want more children (Mamdani, 1973), especially in situations where a large percentage of children die before attaining a productive age. In Chichimila, families with many children are considered happy families. It is difficult for people to speak about the ideal family in terms of numbers. When asked how many children one should have to be happy, no one seemed to be able to give a figure. People do not plan to have a certain number of children, because they believe that children are born by God's will.

"LA COMIDA NO ALCANZA PARA TODOS." (There is not enough food for everybody.) This motto, on a poster showing a large family and an empty plate, hangs on the wall of the rural clinic in Chichimila. The Mexican govenment has made an effort to convince the Maya, and other Indian groups, to limit the size of their families. The villagers understand that there are problems feeding and clothing a family with many children. But they believe that difficulties exist only while their children are infants. After the initial period of growing up, children are easy to care for because they can now start helping each other and helping their parents. Children are security for one's old age, and they can make a great contribution to a family's collective labor. Most of all, they are a source of happiness. Some informants said that a woman with no children would suffer in her old age because she would not have anyone to care for her. Childless people also worry whether anyone will take care of their funerals and the religious rituals connected with them. One woman said that one can probably rely on a niece or a nephew for help, but there is no one like one's own child in this connection. Sons and daughters are believed to be characteristically patient with their old parents. Some said that if a person has many children at least a few of them will turn out to be helpful and look after their old parents. A person with no children is thought to have a higher probability of becoming a beggar in old age. In Mayan culture, the dead and the living are always connected. In Chichimila, children are not excluded from funerals. I saw children of every age at funerals, little ones crying because their mothers were crying, children six years and older playing and watching what was being done at the burial of the deceased.

In November, In Yucatan everyone performs ceremonies for the *Dia de Difuntos* (The Day of The Dead) on November 22. During the whole month, the spirits of the dead are believed to come to earth to visit their families. Each family that has deceased parents or children prepares food, usually the best food, such as tamales, *relleno negro* (pork with some spices and burnt peppers), and other dishes as well as the favorite food of the deceased. Each family arranges an altar in a corner of their room and puts some of the cooked food in bowls and other favorite items of the deceased such as cigarettes for a man or flowers for a woman. The family members get together and pray in front of the altar once or twice a day. Neighbors and friends get together to celebrate and food is exchanged. During this month, members of families go to visit the cemetery where their relatives are buried and put flowers on the tombs. The celebration on November 22 is recognized by the state; consequently, all government and business offices are closed, but the celebration in the villages continues for the entire month of November. During this month, people slaughter their pigs and turkeys. Some people are left with no animals after the celebration and must begin raising some animals for the next year's *Dia de Difuntos*.

Throughout November, the spirits of the dead are expected to come at night and eat. If no one has prepared food for them, it is believed that they go in the kitchen and prepare it themselves. There is no fear of the spirits of the deceased. Villagers believe that they will not harm anyone even if their family neglects them and fails to prepare food. However, sons and daughters themselves feel responsible for ensuring that the appropriate ceremonies are performed for their deceased parents. In addition to leaving food out on the altar, people in Chichimila also put food in baskets or gourds, which they hang outside their homes. This food is for the spirits of those people who did not have children. In November, when all the dead come to visit, the childless ones are assumed to wander in the village, not having any children to visit, and the ones with children are expected to provide food for the wandering spirits. Furthermore, it is assumed that people without children become beggars in old age because they have no one to care for them and that this form of life continues even after death, so that these spirits return to visit as beggars. The importance of children in Mayan society goes beyond security for old age. There is a continuous responsibility and commitment between children and parents.

In a society where there is a great emphasis on fecundity and where the infant mortality rate is still high, the fertile woman is the most preferred and contraceptives are not used. Uncertainty and the high rate of infant mortality are major factors in the common practice of bearing as many children as possible to ensure at least a few survivors.

Data from Chichimila indicate that the average age of marriage of women in the study was 18.6 (SD 4.5), with ages ranging between 13 and 40. Because they did not use any birth control methods, many were pregnant at regular two-year intervals. The average number of pregnancies for the women in the sample was seven, with an average of 4.7 children surviving the first year of life. Women married early and continued to have children until menopause. Women continued to give birth even after their children were married. In Chichimila, it is common to see mother and daughter pregnant at the same time. In fact, women generally report that their last menstrual cycle coincided with their last pregnancy.

Most women breast-feed their children until they reach one and one-half to two years of age. Some women felt that breast-feeding helped to space their pregnancies. A long period of amenorrhea following childbirth is considered normal and most of the women say that they did not get back on their cycle for approximately one and one-half years after they gave birth. Many women report having few or no periods between pregnancies. One woman said that she did not have her period for fifteen years due to successive pregnancies and long periods of amenorrhea.

Overall, Mayan women viewed pregnancy as a dangerous and stressful experience. When they were asked about their pregnancies, many women reported being anxious and recalled their pregnancy symptoms in detail. More than one-half of the women said that they had nausea and vomiting, lost their appetites during the first trimester of their pregnancies, and experienced fatigue and backaches toward the last part of their pregnancies. Only 6 percent of the women had bleeding while pregnant. In general, pregnancy symptoms such as nausea and vomiting were considered natural and temporary, and women tolerated the discomfort without seeking any medical help.

A pregnant woman performs all the necessary activities to maintain her household. It is believed that a pregnant woman who sits around too much will have a hard labor. For example, one of my informants continually nagged her daughter-in-law to keep moving in the last month of her pregnancy, even though the young woman felt tired most of the time and preferred to stay in her hammock. Fifty-five percent of the women said that they had easy labor in all of their pregnancies,

23 percent had variable experiences, and 22 percent had difficult labor, of whom some had to be taken to a physician in Valladolid. Seventy-nine percent of the women gave birth at home with the help of a local midwife; 12 percent stated that they delivered with a doctor's help in at least one of their pregnancies; the balance had only family help.

Greek Women

The average age of marriage for the Greek women in the study was 24.4 (SD 5.0), with ages ranging between 14 and 39; approximately one-half married after age 25. The average pregnancy rate was 2.9 (SD 1.9), with 2.5 children surviving the first year of life. Most of the women in the study came from a family of five to seven surviving children, however, they decided to have only two to three children themselves. This is not because children are less important in Stira than any other peasant community; rather, the depression of the 1930s and the famine and hardship during and after World War II had an impact on the fertility pattern of the rural Greek villages. In Greece, the years from 1930 to 1950 marked a serious rundown of social and economic activities and the rural areas were hit hard. Marriages were reduced to a minimum and girls did not get married until their late twenties or early thirties. These hard years were responsible for bringing a break between the old values and the new, a turning point when the Greek communities as a whole departed from the old way of life (which valued large family size among other things) to new economic and social conditions (du Boulay, 1974).

The sample of women in the study belong to a cohort that went through the hardship of the war and its accompanying famine as young children. The women reported that when they were growing they ate onions, wild greens, bread, and olives. Meat was a very rare food item. All the siblings slept on the floor in a row, walked barefoot, and if the household had a pair of shoes, the girls in the family took turns wearing them to church. One had to sell eggs in order to buy a candle to light at church. There was no cash, and life was very hard. In those days, a favored bride was one who was strong and mature and could work hard in the fields and add to the family's labor force.

The decision of Greek women to have a small family was totally based on economic reasons. They said that they did not have any money in those days and could not afford to bring up more than two children. Besides, after 1950, school attendance of children increased. Although education is free in Greece, one has to provide all the necessary books and supplies for the children, as well as clothing and shoes. These extra expenses were hard to meet if a family had more than two children. The parents wanted to provide their children with what they did not have themselves as children. Some women mentioned that now their children are grown, they would have liked to have one more child. Especially those with only daughters regret their decision to have only two children. These women feel that the third pregnancy would have produced a son to carry on the family name.

In order to keep their families small, Greek women practice birth control. The most common birth control method in Greece is abortion, which is true in both urban and rural areas. However, because of religious beliefs and fear of village gossip, no woman wants others to know how many abortions she has had. A 75-year-old woman told me that she had two abortions when she was young. Because her sons were already teenagers her pregnancies were considered inappropriate for her age. Two days later, this woman came to the house where I stayed and told the landlady, who was her friend, to ask me not to tell anyone about her abortions. She was afraid that she would be the subject of gossip for something that happened about 40 years ago.

Because the decision with regard to family size is the responsibility of the man as well as the woman, the men use condoms. Rural Greeks also followed sexual taboos: one should not have sex on Wednesdays and Fridays; no sex during Lent; a man should not sleep with his wife the night before he fills the wine barrels; if one wanted to go to church, he or she should not have sex the night before Sunday, or a saint's day. The combination of condoms, abortions, and sex taboos enables the villagers to limit their families to two to three children.

However, most grandparents do not like the fact that their children are having two children. They particularly do not like the idea of having only one child. They said, "one is no better than none." If something happens to the child, there will be no way to replace him or her, but if one has three or four children, there would at least be some left. One elderly woman said that she did not feel it was economic hardship that made it hard to raise more children; rather, it was the fault of the women. The women did not want to work hard and preferred to buy everything ready-made. There would not be enough money if one wanted to buy everything and raise a large family as well. Thus, many feel the women are to blame if they are not productive and helpful in the household economy.

The value of children in the Greek community is no different than in the Mayan culture. Although people had small families, they still expected their children to take care of them when they grow old. The

Greeks seemed to be forced to change due to different social and economic factors that were beyond their control, and now they could not go back to the old ways. They were very much aware that their children would be leaving them for the urban life once they grew up. Some of the older people are already experiencing the hardship of old age alone because their children could not be close by to help. Thus, as described above, some of them expressed anxiety and concern about their well-being in old age.

The sample of women in the Greek study were the first generation that started limiting their families' size. In Greece, family planning is left to the individual; the government did not have any major influence. Greek women did not seem physically stressed from too many pregnancies or long periods of lactation because they breast fed only six to nine months. Rather, stress for Greek women was caused by constant worry about unwanted pregnancy. In Greek culture, age and appropriate life stage is very important. For example, a woman would feel very embarrassed if she gave birth to a child at the same time her daughter or daughter-in-law did so. Moreover, it is embarrassing for a teenage boy to see his mother pregnant, because it reveals the sexuality of the mother. When Kiria Vasula was pregnant with her last child, her eldest son was 13 years old. She stated that her son cried when he found out about her pregnancy because he was afraid of being ridiculed by his friends. This was an accident and the mother continued the pregnancy even though it was a culturally embarrassing situation. Another woman said that she cried the whole time she was pregnant with her last child. Because it was an accident, she was caught among the moral issues of abortion, the villagers' gossip, and her embarrassment about having a child in old age.

A planned pregnancy within the appropriate age seemed to have no particular problems associated with it. Among the women, two-thirds said that they did not worry about their health during their pregnancies. The discomfort and symptoms associated with pregnancy were considered natural and among those who reported such symptoms as nausea or vomiting, nearly nine out of ten did nothing to alleviate the problem, a few treated themselves, and fewer than 10 percent said they went to a doctor. Women worked hard throughout pregnancy. One-half of the women reported easy labor; one-quarter had a variable experience, and one-quarter had a difficult labor. The majority of the women gave birth in a clinic outside of the village, in Athens, Karistos, or Halkida. About one-quarter said they gave birth at home with the help of a physician. Only one woman had had all her babies at home with the help of a traditional midwife.

9

Comparing Reproductive Histories, Part II: Menopause in Two Cultures

The disease model of menopause in Western industrialized societies has been developed from the experience of medical practitioners
and biomedical theory and is based on evidence gathered from women
who *seek* medical help; consequently, it is appropriate to begin by comparing the views about menopause held by medical practioners,
themselves often trained in Western biomedicine, who served the Mayan
and Greek population studied.

Dr. Rodriges is a 70-year-old physician living in Valladolid, who
is consulted most by Chichimila villagers. He has been practicing
medicine for 40 years at the same location. For many years, he was the
only doctor in town. Most of his clients are drawn from the villages
around Valladolid and some come from as far as Chan Kom, about 60
kilometers away. Passing by his clinic often on my way to and from
Chichimila, I observed that it was always crowded. At times, his waiting
room was so full that clients had to sit outside on the pavement, waiting
their turns. Because he saw Mayan women of all ages, he was an excellent
source of information on Mayan women's health, particularly for
information about their reproductive cycles.

Dr. Rodriges contends that menopause does not present a life crisis,
psychological, or physiological problems for Mayan village women.
Mayan women associate menstruation with illness and look forward to
the time when they no longer have menses. Sickness aside, they also

feel that menstruation is bothersome and worry about staining their garments. During his work in Valladolid, he estimates that only 3 percent of the menopausal women he treated complained of hot flashes. A few of the menopausal women he treated complained of frequent menses and increased menstrual flow. He claimed that once a Mayan woman learned the cause of her condition, she never returns for treatment.

Other physicians working in the regional hospital in Valladolid were in general agreement with Dr. Rodriges. These physicians were: Dr. Gomez, director of the hospital; Doctora Luci, epidemiologist; and Dr. Lopez, a general practitioner in charge of obstetrics and gynecology in the hospital. Dr. Lopez also was the head of a Protestant clinic in Xochenpich, a Mayan village, about an hour's drive from Valladolid. Interviews and discussions with these physicians indicated that the most frequent problem among the Mayan women was pregnancy complications. The women get married early and do not use contraceptives, some of them from ignorance, some because of religion, and some because their husbands want more children. They never saw women with complaints that arose due to menopause.

On one occasion while I was interviewing Dr. Lopez, he invited me to go with him to the delivery room where a woman was waiting. The woman in the delivery room was 37 years old and had edema. She had had 17 pregnancies, and had eight living children. Dr. Lopez said that most pregnant Mayan women have anemia and edema, conditions that are dangerous for both the mother and the fetus, and that some women die from these complications. By contrast, he asserted categorically that the problems associated with menopause elsewhere are unknown here. According to him, women think about it only to the extent that it means they can no longer have children. He also said that the women do not understand the physiological changes associated with menopause; they think of this stage in their lives as a normal transition. Some older women complain of headaches, muscle aches, and rheumatism; these usally occur after the age of menopause and according to Dr. Lopez, women do not connect these symptoms with menopause. When I asked Dr. Lopez if osteoporosis is common in older women in the villages, he replied that there is no particular problem of bone fracture associated only with older women among the population.

While we were discussing these issues, Dr. Lopez interrupted the conversation and went into the delivery room to help the woman in labor. After the delivery, the discussion continued with all three physicians at the director's office. A few minutes later, another doctor walked in and was introduced to me as the physician in charge of preventive medicine. All joined in the discussion, agreeing that psychological and phsiological problems due to menopause are unknown among Mayan village women. They claimed that Mayan cultural taboos are associated only with menstruation and there are no Mayan old wives' tales or taboos related to menopause. Doctora Luci said that menopause is considered by Mayan village women as a very tranquil and calm stage . in a woman's life.

According to the physicians interviewed, the major problem of the Mayan population is malnutrition. The physician in preventive medicine said that villagers are not used to eating vegetables and fruit. Their diet consists of corn, beans, and rice, although most of the time it is just corn and beans because they could not afford to buy rice often. Meat is rarely eaten, sometimes a few eggs are available, and Coca-Cola has become a main drink in the villages. Causes of morbidity in villages are malnutrition, pneumonia, anemia, tuberculosis, parasites, and diarrhea. INI health survey reports prepared in 1981 confirm the physicians' statements concerning these illnesses. There had also been a few cases of malaria and hepatitis, the physicians noted, and dengue fever is common in the area from September through December.

The hospital social worker, Señorita Angelita, was also interviewed, and her answers agreed with the physicians'. Her main job is promoting the family planning program, and she works with Mayan village women in the area. She claimed that none of the Mayan women she came in contact with reported illnesses or symptoms associated with menopause and feels that generally they have no preoccupation with menopause.

The other sources of information on menopause were the village midwives, local healers, and the participants themselves. Doña Conchita, one of the three midwives in Chichimila, in addition to midwifry, treats women who have problems with their cycle and infertility. Her clients are mainly of reproductive age. Menopausal women do not go to her for consultation because, according to Doña Conchita, there are no special problems associated with this stage in a woman's life. She stated that she could tell the difference between a pregnant woman and a menopausal one by palpating and examining the womb and the ovaries. She said that when a woman approaches menopause her periods become diminished and irregular and gradually stop. Some women hemorrhage and, instead of delayed periods, have frequent flow. She expressed no knowledge of any other problem associated with menopause.

Doña Conchita herself married at age 12, gave birth to 13 children, of whom six are living, and had menopause at age 40. She did not remember any effect other than the actual cessation of her menses. I asked her if women felt any different, if they felt *bochorno* (sudden sensation of heat), or complained of not feeling good, and if they were expected to show any unusual behavior at the age of menopause. Doña Conchita seemed puzzled by my questions. She could not understand why I was probing to find out if women had any discomfort or problems at this stage. She thought that I was trying to tell her that menopause was abnormal, so she threw the question back at me and wanted to know about women where I lived.

I explained to her that menopause happens to all women but it is experienced differently in other cultures, and I wanted to know how Mayan women experience menopause. I also mentioned that a woman in America might have her period as late as age 50 or 55. Doña Conchita said women in America must have many children then. When I told her that they usually only have two children, she was surprised.

Besides Doña Conchita, other midwives, older women, Mayan men, and local healers were interviewed. They all indicated that the only recognized symptom of menopause was irregularity and final cessation of the menses.

One of the Mayan men interviewed was a 40-year-old man, Don Fernando, who lives with his wife and children in a nearby village and works at the INI library in Valladolid. He has lived in the village his entire life and claims that he has never heard of problems related to menopause. He said that older women know about herbs to regulate menstruation and to abort pregnancy, but menopause was unrecognized and there was no expectation of behavioral change during menopause. Generally, his statements agreed with information gathered from the *h-men* Don Antonio and the *curandero* Don Nacho. This suggests that Mayan village women do not exhibit behavorial changes at menopause nor present physiological complaints particularly associated with this stage of life to medical or health practitioners.

What experiences of or beliefs about menopause did women in the study have who did *not* seek the assistance of any medical or practioners or local healers? I asked all the women in the study sample what they anticipate at the age of menopause; their attitudes toward menopause; how they perceived the experiences of menopausal women in Chichimila; and any behavior particularly associated with menopausal women. Menopausal and postmenopausal women in the study were asked about their own experience of menopause, the symptoms associated with menopause, and how they felt and what they believed their health status to be before and after menopause. All women in the study indicated that Mayan women did not associate menopause with physical or emotional symptomatology. None reported that they had hot flashes or cold sweats.

The survey data indicate that the average reported age for onset of menopause for the menopausal and postmenopausal women in the study was 42, with ages ranging between 33 and 55. For the sample group, the onset of menopause was clustered between the ages of 35 and 45 (see Table 5). Seven percent of the women had menopause between ages 30 and 35; 35 percent between ages 36 and 40; 42 percent between ages 41 and 45; 11 percent between ages 46 and 50; and only 4 percent between ages 51 and 55. Two-thirds of the women had menopause before age 45 and, of these, almost one-half before age 40.

I also collected information from women in villages other than Chichimila . I visited some of the rural clinics in these villages, and accompanied the doctors and nurses on their house visits. Overall, my Mayan women informants themselves knew that menopause occurs, and the only major change associated in their minds with this event was the cessation of menstruation and the end of fertility. The Mayan informants did not have a special term for this: they referred to it simply as the time a woman stops menstruating for good ("cuando se acaba la regla por completo").

The Mayan women perceived menopause as an event that occurs when a woman has used up all her blood, that is, menstrual blood. Thus, they believed that the onset of menopause occurs early for those women who have had many children because they had used up their blood by giving birth often. When one of the women in the sample was asked if she still had her period she looked at me with surprise and said, "How do you expect me to have any more? Didn't you see how many children I have? It was all used up. What's more, the blood is finally used up, because of giving birth to so many children." This was a 45-year-old woman who had 12 pregnancies, of which eight children survived. She was menopausal at 37.

Efforts were made to elaborate what the sensation of *bochorno* might be, but the Mayan women responded that they did not have any sensations of heat associated with menopause. One could say that because the temperature in Yucatan is generally hot, it might be that the women did, indeed, have hot flashes, but were unable to differentiate the sensation of heat within the body (hot flashes) from the outside temperature. However, the women do recognize temperature changes in their body such as fever, *calentura*, due to illnesses. A mother puts her hand on her child's forehead to see if he or she has a high temperature whenever she suspects that the child might not be feeling well. In addition, although the temperature in Yucatan is often high, evenings are cool and, because the Mayan *paja* hut does not retain heat, it is comfortable at night. They also have cold evenings from October until January. If the Mayan women had hot flashes, they could certainly recognize the change in their body heat at night when it is cool, especially because hot flahses are supposed to be more frequent at night.

Because many women are married at ages thirteen or fourteen, it was not uncommon to find women age 35 to 40 who were already grandmothers; some women continue bearing children after becoming grandmothers. Thus, in Chichimila, the role of grandparenthood does not necessarily coinside with the onset of menopause. Furthermore, the loss of fertility at menopause is not lamented because a woman feels she had already produced enough children. The women also felt that early menarche meant early menopause, and late menarche meant late menopause. Women with one or no children were expected to have later menopause. Their explanation was that because these women have not had many children, their blood should last longer than those who have had many births. Most of all, my informants felt that an unmarried woman should have her cycle longer than any of the married women, because not only has she not used up her blood, she has also not lost her strength through the agony and stress of pregnancy and childbearing so that her body is still intact and strong. Indeed, the married women with one child or none and the single women did seem to have relatively late onset of menopause. However, the sample is not large enough to judge the significance of this observation. When women were asked at what age a woman should expect to have her menses stop, they were very much aware that this would not happen at the same age for everyone, and stated that it could occur any time after age 30, depending on how many children one had, as well as the age of the onset of menarche. Above all, they felt it depended on God's will, because the number of children one has is a gift of God.

My interviews of Mayan women in the study sample agree with the opinions of the health professionals interviewed in Valladolid and the village. These Mayan women perceive menopause as a life stage free of taboos and restrictions, and offering increased freedom of movement.

Thus some of the women's statements (translated) were: "Finally the time has come: it's better this way." "We are happy that we do not have any more because we have time to visit." "It is not like before; I did not go out because of it." The women also said they felt relieved at the cessation of the monthly menstrual flow which was considered bothersome, and menopause represented a relief from the anxiety of accidents and staining their white garments. Women stated, "I did not like to make tortillas when I had my period because I was afraid that I would stain my dress."

Women were asked what their husbands felt now that they were menopausal, and most said that their husbands were indifferent. One woman said, "It does not matter to him because we have already enough children." Another woman said, "What more was he to think? He is not the one who menstruates."

Moreover, they claimed better sexual relationships with their husbands after menopause. Because the risk of pregnancy was no longer present, they felt relaxed about sexual activities. They used such phrases as "I am happy that I am not going to be sick, pregnant." "Better because I am not going to have any more children. I am clean." The Mayan women say *esta enferma,* which means she is sick, to express one's state of pregnancy and they say, *se alivia,* which means *she recovered,* when the baby is born. Although the same terminology is used for the state of pregnancy as for other illnesses and recovery, Mayan women are aware of the underlying differences.

In general, women welcomed menopause and associated this stage with being young and free. Many said that they felt as young as a six-year-old girl. When asked to compare menopause with life before they said such things as: "Life is better, because I feel like a little girl." "More content, because this way one can go out and walk around any place." In Mayan culture, the status of a woman is not based on her chronological age alone. Thus, menopause does not bring changes in her household roles.

In addition, although fecundity has a high value in the Mayan culture, by the time a woman attains age 30, she has usually borne numerous children, and by age 35, she often has grandchildren. Thus, a woman does not need any more children at menopause. When menopausal and postmenopausal women in the study were asked if they would have liked to have more children, they stated that they did not need any more; they felt it was time for them to enjoy their grandchildren.

Before my initial interviews with Mayan women, I had casual conversations regarding my work with a few urban, upper-class, middle-aged, Yucatecan Landino women in Merida. I did not have any problem explaining to these women what hot flashes were. Actually they were the ones who introduced me to the word *bochorno*, the Spanish word for *hot flashes*. But my Mayan village informants convinced me that they did not know what hot flashes were. My data from the premenopausal Mayan women in the study indicate that Mayan women do not have preformed cultural knowledge and anticipations relating to the onset of menopause other than the expectation of the cessation of menstruation. Furthermore, the premenopausal Mayan women informants looked forward to the onset of menopause for the reasons described above. However, although there was no awareness of certain symptoms as linked to menopause, some women reported experiences that Western biomedicine and female tradition in other parts of the world see as connected. Most postmenopausal women in the study reported they had irregular menses with a three- to six-month delay for a year or so before termination. A few reported that they had frequent menstrual flow every two weeks and had hemorrhages before finally stopping. It was also common for women to stop menstruating with their last pregnancy and not to have the irregular menses that other women mentioned. For example, when Doña Alejandra was asked whether she still had her period, she said, "No, after the birth of my last child I saw my period just once and then it left me." Some women stated that they had headaches and felt dizzy at times. However, they did not associate these with menopause because headaches and dizziness are common symptoms associated with other ailments. Some women said that they have dizzy spells because they felt weak (*debil*). Some of my Mayan women informants stated that they had been diagnosed by physicians in Valladolid as anemic. In Chichimila, people refer to an anemic condition as *debilidad* (feebleness). Mayan women associate an anemic condition with loss of blood due to frequent childbearing. Based on information gathered from INI and physicians in Valladolid, people in Chichimila have a high rate of anemia and vitamin deficiency to which the headaches and dizziness could be attributable.

At times my own questions regarding menopausal symptoms were returned to me. The local midwives as well as some of the women wanted to know if I thought menopause was an "abnormal" situation happening only among Mayan women. One woman said, "I don't know, my mother was telling me that it would happen to all women." They did not understand why I was probing to find out if women had discomfort or problems at this stage. No one had raised such a question before because the cessation of menses was considered normal for a woman who had borne enough children and there was no discomfort or illness associated with it that they knew about. For Mayan women, every phenomenon that exists could be explained by their customs. Most women said it was Mayan custom that women have many children, they breast-feed, and they have menopause. My informants referred to the way of life and behavior they believe makes them distinct from other groups as "Mayan custom."

The women's responses were not different from those of women in Western cultures on questions concerning symptoms of pregnancy and discomfort and pain associated with menstruation. No one had difficulty understanding what was asked and their answers were detailed.

My data from Chichimila women, physicians, midwives, local healers, and the women themselves indicate that menopause is not a personally or culturally elaborated stage in the life of Mayan women.

In general, Mayan women were concerned with pregnancy and childbirth but not with menopause. The information in this study indicates that Mayan village women welcome menopause, conceive of it as a natural event, and associate this stage with being young and free. They are pleased to be rid of their period, and thus premenopausal women in the study look forward to the onset of menopause.

Although there are conflicting views on the psychosomatic and psychological symptoms of menopause, most Western physicians agree that hot flashes are physiological symptoms, the direct results of estrogen decline at menopause. If menopause is principally a hormonal event, one would expect that women throughout the world would experience similar symptoms. However, none of the Mayan women reported hot flashes; the only physiological change that they recognize is the cessation of menstruation. In addition, my information from traditional Mayan healers and books written on Mayan botanical medicine (Cabrera, 1980; Heath, 1979) indicated that Mayans associate female disorders with the childbearing years. If menopause had been associated with any symptoms of discomfort in the Mayan culture, one would expect midwives and healers who treat women for gynecological complaints to report this; they did not. The information in this study indicates that menopause is not a highly elaborated concept for Mayan village women, and it presents neither a life crisis nor psychological distress nor physiological problems.

Greek Women

The physician in Stira, Dr. Papadopoulos, stated that he does not recall village women coming to see him for menopausal complaints. Most of his services include treatment for colds and flu, food poisoning, and other primary care needs.

As with Mayan women, menopause is a life stage at which a Greek women feels free of taboos and restriction. After the cessation of the menses, a woman could participate fully in church activities. Thus, the women's statements were "a woman is free to go where ever she wants; . . . free to go to church, to make cheese. . .; because when a woman has her period and salts cheese, the cheese spoils." In addition, a postmenopausal woman is freed from being a sexual threat to the community and a potential cause of shame for her family, because she is no longer considered sensual and desirable by other men. As with the Mayan women, the Greek women reported better sexual relationship with their husbands. Because the risk of pregnancy was no longer present, they reported that they felt more relaxed about sexual activities and were relieved from the anxiety of unwanted pregnancy. Thus, the women said, ". . . that it is better this way because one does not have fear of getting pregnant and therefore feels relieved." However, the women also associated menopause with growing old, not having energy, and, generally a downhill life course. Although old age is respected in the Greek culture, growing old is not desired. An older woman wears gray, dark blue, brown, or black. If she is a widow, she wears black all the time. A woman who wears an inappropriate outfit and the wrong colors for her age is criticized by others. For example, one of the women in the village who was in her early fifties, bought a burgundy blouse from a vendor who came to Stira once a week. Even though the color looked nice on her, a week later she exchanged the blouse for a dark blue one because she was afraid that people would ridicule her for wearing a color inappropriate for her age. Women reported that menopause signified that they were no longer in the main stream of the society. Therefore, premenopausal women reported anxiety and a negative attitude in association with menopause and accepted it with mixed feelings.

The average reported age for onset of menopause for the women in the Greek sample was 47, with ages ranging from 32 to 54, and three-quarters of the women were clustered between the ages at 43 to 54 (see Table 5). When asked about the experience of menopausal symptomatology, 73 percent of the menopausal and postmenopausal women reported having had hot flashes and 30 percent cold sweats. Forty-two percent reported headaches, and dizziness, 30 percent insomnia, and 12 percent hemorrhage. Fewer than 2 percent claimed to have experienced irritability and feelings of melancholy. Two-thirds of the women said that they did not see any change in their health due to menopause, while approximately one-third said that they felt weak and got sick more often now than when they were premenopausal.

Menopause is considered by the women to be a natural phenomenon that all women experience. Thus, even though the women reported experiencing hot flashes and cold sweats, I must emphasize that they did not consider these to be disease symptoms. They felt that it was a natural phenomenon causing a temporary discomfort, and did not feel a need to seek medical intervention. Unlike the Mayan women, the Greek women understood what I was asking and with no more explanation the older women told me the Greek word used to express *hot flashes* is *exapsi.* Moreover, not only did they report the experiences of hot flashes, they were able to give detailed accounts of the process, the time they most felt hot flashes, and the sensation and changes in their body. Women said that they felt more hot flashes at night and around the time they usually expected to have their periods. The sensation of heat is usually around their chests and faces. When this happened during the day, they tried to cool themselves and went out in the fresh air. At night, they threw off their covers. One woman said, that when she felt hot in the middle of the night, she threw off the cover, and held to the metal frame of her bed which was cold. For a while, her husband was annoyed at her for waking him in the middle of the night. They said that one gets *exapsi* because the detained blood boils up in the body. When women were asked what they did to relieve hot flashes a typical statement was, "Nothing; it passes on its own." Thus, the only thing women did to alleviate hot flashes was going out in the fresh air and cooling themselves. Hot flashes are expected to end within a year after a woman completely stops having her period.

If menopause occurred at the right age, it was considered a relief from the monthly menstrual flow, which was thought to be bothersome, as well as a relief from unwanted prgenancy. The women realized that the age of onset of menopause differed among individuals. The general belief was that if a woman had early menarche, she would have early menopause and vice versa. Women reported this regardless of their own experience. The women with early menarche were assumed to have started losing their blood early; thus, it was certain to stop early. However, if menopause occurred before age 40, regardless of the early or late onset of menarche, it was expected to create health problems. Thus, women said, "When one is young, it affects the nerves, but when menopause occurs at the right age, there is no problem." Symptoms such as irritability, melancholic feelings, and emotional problems at menopause were thought to be due to premature menopause.

Retention of the unclean blood due to premature menopause was believed to cause a wide range of health problems. Some Greek women reported that it was good to menstruate for a longer period of time because it meant that the blood was being cleaned. With early menopause, they feared a negative health effect because the cleaning was no longer taking place. Thus, one typical remark was, ". . . it is bad if it comes too early because when a woman has her period it cleans her blood, . . . particularly if the woman is young, the unclean blood could go to her head." The Greek women did not expect to menstruate all their lives in order to be healthy, rather they felt that the cleansing was necessary up to a certain age. A 49-year-old woman stated, "I think it is good that I still have my period. My friend Alexandra is the same age as I am, but hers stopped three or four years ago. I don't know why. I think the longer a woman has her period, the better for her health." When the same woman was asked if she would like to continue having her period any longer, she stated that it had been long enough for her, she was tired of having to bother every month, and she would not mind if it stopped soon.

Negative attitudes and anxiety associated with menopause were expressed mostly by premenopausal women. The menopausal and postmenopausal women emphasized more the relief and freedom that menopause offers. Women stated that they did not look forward to onset of menopause, but once it happened they did not feel as bad as they had anticipated. One woman said she was so worried when her period started being irregular, she went to a doctor in Athens and asked him to do anything to make her period regular. However, she said that the doctor discouraged her from having any medical intervention and now it had been more than six months since her period stopped. She said that it was not as bad as she thought. She actually liked it because she did not have to worry about getting pregnant. A few other women who reported that they went to a doctor when their period stopped indicated that the Greek physicians told the women that menopause was a relief, promoted positive attitudes, and did not encourage hormonal therapy.

The two groups of women, Mayan and Greek, show some striking similarities and differences with respect to experience of and attitudes toward menopause. Exploration of the causes and meaning of these patterns follows in Chapter 10.

10

Menopause: A Biocultural Event

The few existing data on menopausal experiences of women in non-Western cultures suggest that menopausal women in Western cultures report more symptoms than women in non-Western cultures. In the cross-cultural literature, the rarity or complete absence of menopausal symptoms in non-Western cultures was thought to be due to the fact that menopause precipitates a positive role change for women in these cultures (Flint, 1975; Griffin, 1977, 1982). A change from high to low status is assumed to correlate with experience of menopause as negative and incapacitating, while improvement and freedom from cultural taboos associated with childbearing years at middle age correlate with positive or indifferent attitudes and thus reports of fewer symptoms (Flint, 1975).

In comparing the menopausal experience of Mayan women with those of women in Western, industrialized cultures, however, one may mistakenly attribute the differences to different attitudinal factors and to gain or loss in status at middle age. In Mayan society, a woman's role change and gains in status do not correlate with menopausal age. As described earlier, a woman's status in Mayan society does not depend solely on her chronological age. Rather, it is a result of an interrelation of factors such as age and the marital status of her sons, both of which are independent of onset of menopause.

The data suggest the following hypothesis instead: the Mayans' positive attitude towards menopause and aging accounts for the lack of psychological symptoms in the Mayan women as compared to Western women. But the hypothesis does *not* explain the absence of hot flashes among Mayan women, a symptom said to be due to hormonal changes that are universal. This absence raises a question about the link between hormonal change and hot flashes.

Comparing the menopausal experiences of Western and non-Western women is difficult and gives rise to misleading conclusions if social, economic, and cultural differences are not taken into account. Comparisons of menopausal experiences of women from different non-industrial societies may provide us with the means for distinguishing the physiological, social, and cultural manifestations of menopause.

Comparison of the Reproductive Histories of Mayan and Greek Women

Comparison of the data from these two groups indicate both similarities and some marked differences between women in the two cultures. The women seem to share similar cultural values regarding many beliefs and practices about menstruation and childbearing, but had differences in their childbearing patterns, experiences with menopause, as well as in their diets and the ecological niche in which they lived.

Similarities

The information indicates that women in both cultures were concerned much more with menstruation and factors related to child birth than with menopause. Like Mayan women, the Greeks also have taboos and restrictions related to menstruation and childbearing. For example, rural Greek women believe that menstruation is a curse as a result of Eve's sin. Consequently, among Greek peasants, a menstruating woman and a woman who just gave birth are not allowed to participate in religious activities because they are considered "unclean" and contaminated. Mayans believe that a menstruating woman can cause disaster and induce sickness in a newborn baby. Morever, in both cultures, citrus fruit, cold drinks, and bathing are forbidden during menstruation because they were believed to stop the menstrual flow. Both groups use a variety of herbs to treat menstrual irregularities and different illnesses. Some of these herbs are used by both groups for similar ailments. For example, both Mayans and Greeks used oregano to treat menstrual irregularities.

Women in both cultures perceive menopause as a life stage free of taboos and restriction, which, consequently, offers increased freedom to participate in many activities. For example, Greek women could participate fully in church activities, and Mayan women moved freely without anxiety about inducing sickness in others. Because the risk of pregnancy was no longer present, both groups reported that they felt more relaxed about sexual activities, thereby improving their sexual relationships with their husbands. The women also stated that they felt relieved from the fear of unwanted pregnancies, as well as from the monthly menstrual flow, which was considered bothersome.

The data also indicate that in both cultures, the roles of good mother, housekeeper, and hard worker are highly valued. In both societies, old age is associated with increased power and respect. Particularly for a woman, status increases with age, as her sons marry and establish their own families. The mother-in-law, both in Mayan and Greek culture, occupies the most authoritative position as the head of the extended family households of her married sons. Moreover, older women are believed to possess special healing skills. Therefore, in both Mayan and Greek villages, the older woman of the family is the first to be consulted when a family member gets sick, particularly her grandchildren. In both cultures, healing is one of the older woman's nurturing roles as a mother and as a carrier of old traditions (Campbell, 1964; Blum and Blum, 1965; Elmendorf, 1976; Steggerda, 1941; Redfield, 1941).

Differences

The data also indicate marked differences between the Mayan and Greek women in relation to menopausal experience and childbearing patterns. The average reported age for onset of menarche for both cultures was approximately the same: 13 for Mayan women and 14 for Greek women. However, the average age for onset of menopause was 42 for the Mayans and 47 for the Greeks. With regard to the age for onset of menopause (see Table 5), the age difference between the two groups is quite striking. The Mayan women clustered between the ages of 36 and 45, while the Greek women clustered between the ages of 46 and 55.

Table 4

Comparison of the Distribution of Menstrual Stages of Mayan and Greek Women

	Mayan (N = 107)		Greek (N = 96)	
Menstrual Stages	N	Percent	N	Percent
Premenopausal	36	33.6	30	31.3
Menopausal	36	33.6	31	32.3
Postmenopausal	35	32.7	35	36.5

Table 5
Comparison of the Distribution of Age at Onset of Menopause
For Mayan and Greek Women

	Mayan (N = 71) x = 42.0		Greek (N = 66) x = 47.0	
Age at Onset	N	Percent	N	Percent
30–35	5	7.0	2	3.3
36–40	25	35.3	6	9.0
41–45	30	42.3	19	28.8
46–50	8	11.3	25	37.8
51--55	3	4.2	14	21.1

Moreover, Mayan women did not associate menopause with any physical or emotional symptomatology. The only recognized physiological event associated with menopause is the cessation of menstruation. Among the Mayan women, menopause is welcomed and expressed with such phrases as "being happy," "free like a young girl again," "content and good health." No Mayan woman reported having hot flashes or cold sweats. Anxiety, negative attitudes, health concerns, and stress for Mayan women were associated with the childbearing years, not with menopause. Menopause was not a negatively perceived concept. Women were pleased to get rid of their periods; thus, premenopausal women in the study looked forward to the onset of menopause.

On the other hand, menopausal experiences among rural Greek women seem to bear more resemblance to the experiences of women in Western, industrialized societies. Even though the postmenopausal and menopausal women reported being relieved from the taboos and restrictions of childbearing years at menopause, overall it was perceived negatively by the premenopausal women. The premenopausal women expressed anxiety and anticipated possible health problems with menopause and were not looking forward to its onset. There is respect and status gain for older women in Greek culture, but getting old was perceived by some Greek women as tantamount to dropping out of the main stream of life. Therefore, some Greek women, particularly the premenopausal group, associated menopause with growing old, diminution of energy, and a general downhill course in life. In striking contrast to the Mayan women, Greek premenopausal women reported anxiety and a negative affect in association with menopause.

Greek postmenopausal and menopausal women reported hot flashes and some cold sweats similar to women in Western, industrialized societies (see Table 6). Greek women, however, differed from women from Western, industrialized countries in their perceptions and management of menopausal hot flashes. Greek women did not perceive hot flashes as a disease symptom and did not seek medical intervention. While they had a variety of herbs to treat menstrual pain and discomfort, they had none for hot flashes. They felt that it was a natural phenomenon causing a temporary discomfort that would stop with no intervention. Symptoms such as irritability, melancholia, and emotional problems were not expected in the normal process of menopause; these symptoms were said to appear only with premature menopause, that is, if it occurred before age 40.

Table 6
Comparison of the Distribution of Menopausal Symptoms for
Mayan and Greek Women

	Mayan (N = 71)		Greek (N = 66)	
Menopausal Symptoms	*N*	*Percent*	*N*	*Percent*
Headache	22	31.0	28	42.4
Dizziness	25	35.2	28	42.4
Hot flashes	0	0	48	72.7
Cold sweats	0	0	20	30.3
Hemorrhage	13	18.3	8	12.1
Insomnia	0	0	20	30.3
Irritable	0	0	10	15.2
Melancholia	0	0	3	3.0

Conclusions

This comparison suggests that the existence or lack of physiological symptoms cannot be explained in terms of role changes at midlife or by the removal of cultural taboos. Greek women and Mayan women in the study seemed to share similar cultural values regarding beliefs and practices of menstruation and childbearing, but have very different menopausal experiences. If menopausal hot flashes and osteoporosis are hormonally induced physiological phenomena, differences in their occurrence should be related to cultural and environmental factors that could affect the production of a hormone such as estrogen. Two such factors could be the diet and fertility patterns which showed such striking differences in the two cultures. In the following, I consider these two factors, diet and fertility patterns, as possible explanations for the variation between the Greek and Mayan women in the experiences of the physiological symptom of menopause, namely, hot flashes.

Hypothesis

Mayan and Greek women differed strikingly in their diet and in their childbearing patterns. Could the differences between their actual experience of menopause in the sense of physiological phenomena be related to these differences? The question is how do childbearing patterns and diet affect reproductive hormones, and in turn, how do such hormones affect the appearance of the physiological phenomena?

For Mayan women, pregnancy was a stressful experience. Because they did not use any birth control, many were pregnant at regular two-year intervals. They married early and continued to bear children until menopause. They all breast-fed their children until they attained age one and one-half or two. Mayan women rarely had a steady menstrual cycle because successive pregnancies and long periods of amenorrhea due to lactation were so common. Unlike Mayan women, Greek women had few pregnancies; they married in their late twenties or early thirties, used birth control, and planned their family size. They breast-fed only six to nine months, and they tended to have steady menstrual cycles.

Moreover, these two cultures also differed in their ecology, which affects diet. The Mayans live in a semitropical environment, a lowland with poor soil, and used a slash-and-burn technique of farming. The climate in Chichimila is generally humid and hot, with temperatures sometimes reaching 110°F. On the other hand, the Greeks live in a rugged mountainous area. The climate in the Greek village varies among seasons: it has short, cold winters with temperatures at times below freezing; temperate, mild springs and falls; and summers with highs of only 80°F. Even though the land cannot be called fertile, the small plots of land that the Greeks use for farming have more top soil than that of the Mayans. Finally, the Greeks have draft animals and produce a greater variety of foods than do the Mayans.

Another striking difference between the two cultures is their diets. The Mayan diet consists of corn, beans, tomatoes, *chaya* (a green leafy plant), some radishes, squash, *camote* (sweet potatoes), very little animal protein, and no milk products. The Mayans are reported to have a high incidence of vitamin deficiency and anemia (Balam, 1981). Greeks, on the other hand, have a wide variety of nutrients: wheat, cheese, milk, eggs, olives, a variety of wild greens, legumes, plenty of meat and fish, fruit, and wine.

Diet

The important role that diet plays in growth and development is well-documented. Poor nutrition allied with chronic infections before puberty is known to have a permanent affect on stature. Malnutrition during childhood slows down skeletal development and delays sexual maturity, such as the onset of menarche in girls. For example, menarche is reported to be earlier in women from well-off families than those from underprivileged families. The number of children in a family and its social class have also been related to the onset of menarche because these variables correlate with nutritional status (Frish et al., 1974; Eveleth and Tanner, 1976). It has been documented that nutrition plays a role in reproduction: it affects conception, fetal mortality, and health of the newborn, and the length of pospartum susceptibility. As Frish (1974) asserts, poor nutrition delays menarche, lengthens the period of adolescent sterility and postpartum amenorrhea, and lowers fecundity.

Not only is the onset of menarche related to a woman's nutritional status, but menstrual activity continues to be affected by nutritional factors throughout a woman's reproductive life. In premenopausal women, the regularity of the menstrual cycle is controlled by neurotransmitters and levels of biogenic amines. However, environmental changes such as fasting or excessive weight loss can inhibit cycling, ovulation, and pituitary response to luteinizing-releasing hormone and thyrotropin-releasing hormone. Thus diet, through modification of brain function as measured by electro-encephalographic activity and sleep patterns or by direct action alters hormone metabolism (Hill et al., 1980; Merimee and Fineberg, 1974; Akesode, Migeon, and Kowarski, 1977; Hurd, Palumbo, and Gharib, 1977).

Differences in hormone production between populations have been partly accounted for by differences in diet (MacMahon et al., 1974). It has also been reported that diet affects ovarian function and adrenal activity, which could be increased by a high protein diet. Hill and his associates (1977) compared Japanese women with Caucasian women and concluded that different populations of comparable age might also have different plasma level of hormones and that dietary factors, such as dietary fat intake, influence the hormone profile in women.

In another study of diet and menstrual activity, Hill and his associates (1980) compared South African black women with North

American white women and concluded that the groups had different hormonal balances during the menstrual cycle. These hormonal differences are assumed to be related to genetic or environmental factors or to both of them. The South African black women maintained a diet high in carbohydrates supplemented with vegetable protein with low fat content. They were shorter and heavier in stature than the white women and maintained greater physical activity in their daily lives. Because physical activities such as running and aerobic exercises are also known to modify androgen metabolism (Kuppasalmi et al., 1976), Hill and his colleagues assumed that the differences in hormonal activity between the South African black women and North American white women could be partially explained by differences in their levels of activity. However, a study of premenopausal and postmenopausal black South African women on a Western-type diet indicated hormonal changes different from the pattern associated with the high carbohydrate diet, which suggests that diet has the primary effect on pituitary activity.

Another study (Hill et al., 1976) also indicates that urbanization and Westernization may also produce changes in the hormone secretion in women through changes in diet. These studies indicate that nutritional patterns and the amount of animal fat consumed and body weight (Frish, 1980) may influence hormone production.

Certainly, diet varies dramatically between the groups of Mayan and Greek women studied. Improvement in the diet of the rural Greek villages in the last two decades has resulted in the disappearance of marked nutritional deficiencies in Greece. For example, pellagra, which appeared before the war in hundreds of cases yearly in Greece, is not seen now (May 1963). Protein malnutrition is seldom seen and severe cases of nutritional deficiency are rare in Greece.

The cultural practices of nutritional intake and ecological as well as economic limitations are major factors in the differences in diet between these two cultures. Although both groups are agrarian, differences exist in the ecological niches they inhabit and the types of food substances that they produce and consume. As discussed before, the Mayans live in a semitropical climate where the only method of farming is slash-and-burn. Their diet consists mainly of corn and beans. Overall, Yucatan is known to have poor soil and the few areas of land that are relatively arable are owned by the middle-class Ladinos who use the land to raise livestock for profit. In recent years, the Eastern part of Yucatan (Tizimin and Panaba), which was mainly a maize growing zone, has been affected by the expansion of private land ownership, *parvifundismo* (Balam, 1981). The Mayan peasants have been pushed off their communal lands to farm on poor soil while the semirich soil is used to grow feed for livestock.

Nutritional research in Latin America indicates that the proportion of maize and beans typically used by Latin Americans for meal combinations provides optimum amino acid complementarity for the two grains when they are eaten together (Maffia, 1974). A national nutritional survey in Mexico (May and McLellan, 1972) indicated that because of the large amount consumed by the rural communities, corn is responsible not only for 70 to 80 percent of the energy supplied, but also for a large percentage of proteins, fats, and vitamins, especially thiamine. This survey also concluded that meat is not very commonly eaten in the rural parts of Mexico. Therefore, animal protein accounts only for 22.9 grams of the total 71.9 grams of protein. Carbohydrates and starches provide 75.2 percent of the calories, protein 14.5 percent and fats 10.3 percent. The protein comes mainly from corn and beans. Animal protein is in short supply and of low quality. Moreover, nutritional anemia is common in rural Mexico, in spite of an adequate level of iron in the diet. This is believed to be the consequence of malabsorption or losses due to parasites. Chavez and Rosado (1967) also found that in Merida, the state capital of Yucatan, 50 percent of the children examined showed signs of malnutrition. Overall, the survey found that the most important clinically expressed nutritional deficiency problems in Mexico are the result of riboflavin, niacin, and protein deficiencies.

Despite the balanced nutrient value of the average Mexican diet, the Mayans' social and economic position, together with the poor nature of the soil, an unpredictable ecosystem, the prevalence of parasites, and the large family size, make it difficult to have enough corn and beans to meet the nutritional demands for an individual. In Chichimila, my observation was that people use few beans in their bean soup. Dishes such as *frijol colado* (mashed bean soup) were rarely prepared by most households because they require large amounts of beans. Most households eat their tortillas with a soup made from a few beans and water.

Because diet affects growth, development, and hormone production, malnutrition should be one of the variables studied in relation to the relatively early onset of menopause for Mayan women. In addition, the effect of the Mayan diet on menopausal symptomatology in general needs further investigation.

Furthermore, information from physicians providing services to both Greek and Mayan villages indicates that in neither culture does osteoporosis appear to be a problem. The mineral contents of the nutrients that these people eat and their daily physical activities also must be studied in relation to osteoporosis. Even though the Mayan diet is deficient in protein, people get an adequate supply of calcium derived from tortillas and from drinking water. For example, the lime water used to soak maize before grinding it into *masa* for tortillas, a practice common to the Mayans and other Latin American peoples, provides the needed calcium in the diet. A Mexican gets more than 500 mgs. of calcium per day from tortillas alone (Cravioto et al., 1945). Mayans also obtain calcium from their drinking water because of the abundant lime in their soil.

Green vegetables are also a source of calcium. One of the prominent newspapers in Yucatan, *Diario de Yucatan*, (1981) had a profile on *chaya:* "El Mal de Huesos y La Chaya" ("Bone Illness, Osterporosis, and Chaya"). This article stated that a United States physician, Everett Smith, recommended that his readers eat *chaya,* a green leafy plant, as a means of preventing osteoporosis. *Chaya* is known to be a rich source of calcium and Vitamin A and it is one of the very few green vegetables that the Maya eat often.

The Greeks also have calcium in their diet from their use of milk and cheese, as well as from their drinking water. In the West, some physicians prescribe both high dietary intake of calcium and physical exercise as a way of preventing osteoporosis (Noridn, 1982; Bachmann, 1984). In addition to their dietary calcium intake, both Mayan and Greek village women of all ages maintain a high level of physical activity. They perform rigorous work at home and in the fields and walk long distances.

Fertility Patterns

A striking difference between the Mayan and Greek women is their fertility patterns. As discussed before, Mayan women marry early, have successive pregnancies, and experience long periods of amenorrhea (because of prolonged lactation coupled with malnutrition). Therefore, Mayan women rarely experience a regular menstrual cycle.

The Mayan fertility pattern is typical of most nonindustrialized, traditional societies. For example, data from the !Kung hunters and gatherers in the Kalahari Desert suggest that given the fertility patterns of traditional societies, a woman would experience about 15 years of lactational amenorrhoea and about 48 menstrual cycles during her entire reproductive life, equivalent to four years (Konner and Worthman, 1980). On the other hand, a woman in an industrialized society with a family size of two children, little or no breast feeding, and a short period of postpartum amenorrhoea (McNeilly, 1979), can expect 35 of her 37 reproductive years to have consistent menstrual cycles (Short, 1978).

Short (1978) also suggests that the reproductive patterns of the traditional, simple societies, such as those of the hunter-gatherer, most likely represent the situation to which human genes are best adapted. Therefore, because no evidence is found of a fundamental change in the reproductive biology of humans in millions of years, there may be significant biological consequences of the present low fertility pattern of women in industrialized societies. The phenomenon of estrogen dependency or deficiency at menopause also may be a result of the change in the reproductive pattern of women in modern industrialized societies. One hypothesis is that decreased childbearing with short periods of lactation and postpartum amenorrhoea possibly expose the body to more estrogenic stimulation and its sudden decline could be manifested in both hot flashes and bone density loss, or in just one of these phenomena.

Furthermore, repeated pregnancies and lactation are known to lead to frequent interruption in cyclic ovarian function (Neville, 1983). For example, during pregnancy, the serum concentration of estrogens and total progestrone levels are high. However, during lactation basal prolactin levels are elevated and progestron and estrogens are suppressed (Martin and Hoffman, 1983). Studies on lactation and hormone levels also indicate that prolactin levels of lactating women are high where breast milk forms all or a substantial portion of infant's diet (Madden at al., 1979; Konner and Worthman, 1980).

Women are usually infertile at least for four to eight weeks after the birth of an infant. However, lactation is known to prolong the infertility period due to the suppression of ovarian activity as a result of high levels of basal prolactin brought about by frequent suckling (McNeilly, 1979). The duration of lactational infertility varies considerably from one society to another, being as short as two to three months in Western, industrialized societies, and as long as three years in the !Kung hunters and gatherers (Simpson-Herbert and Huffman, 1981). The existing evidence suggests that high levels of prolactin appears to have direct interference with ovarian steroid production (McNatty, Sawers, and Sharpe, 1974). Some believe that frequent suckling stimulus itself may be a factor in lactational infertility; however, whether it is prolactin alone or suckling stimulation or both, the fact is that ovulation is suppressed during lactation. For women in industrialized societies where the childbearing rate is low and breast feeding of short duration, the chances of exposure to high levels of prolactin and its biochemical effect is decreased.

The only biological effect of high levels of prolactin that we know about is amenorrhea. However, the adverse effect of continuous exposure of the endometrium and other reproductive tissues of the body to estrogenic stimulation has been documented. For example, estrogen is known to play a major role in the genesis of breast cancer; also postmenopausal women treated with estrogen replacement therapy have a high risk of endometrium carcinoma (Smith et al., 1975; Ziel and Finkle, 1975). Moreover, studies on cancer rates in parous and nulliparous women (Cole et al., 1976) suggest that parity and age at first pregnancey may also alter the estrogen profile.

Although there are no cross-cultural studies specifically concerned with fertility patterns and their effect on bone density loss, some research has peripherally touched on the phenomenon. The few available data suggest that high parity does not predispose to osteoporosis or hip fracture (Gran, 1970; Smith, 1967; Daniell, 1976; Aloia et al., 1983; Wyshak, 1981). Aloia and coworkers (1983) suggest that relatively longer lactation also decreases the risk of osteoporotic fractures; although other studies have shown that lactation is associated with calcium depletion (Atkinson and West, 1970; Wardlaw and Pike, 1986). It has been proposed that reports of osteoporosis in lactating women were probably due to inadequate intake of calcium and vitamin D (Daniell, 1976).

This raises questions about the extent to which frequent interruption in cyclic ovarian function due to successive childbearing, prolonged lactation, and amenorrhoea affect the production of reproductive hormones and the degree to which the latter may affect age at onset of menopause and the presence or absence of hot flashes or even osteoporosis.

Summary

This study has focused on the experience of menopause, its cultural significance and meaning, and its physiological manifestation in peasant women. The findings from this study indicate that the perception and experience of menopause vary among cultures. However, the findings also suggest that cultural factors such as status gain and removal of menstrual taboos are inadequate explanations for cross-cultural variation in the menopausal experiences of women. Besides the social role restrictions and cultural taboos of menstruation, women in nonindustrialized societies have strong similarities in their fertility patterns which in turn may also have effects on the biochemical transformation of the reproductive system.

Like other human developmental events, menopause is a biocultural experience. Therefore, this study points to the fact that research on menopause should consider biocultural factors such as environment, diet, fertility patterns, and exercise levels which could also affect the production and equilibrium of hormones in a woman's body. To do so, more comparisons of menopausal experiences of women from different nonindustrialized societies, as well as within industrialized societies, are needed.

In addition, the data from this study raise significant questions regarding the effect of frequent childbearing patterns and long periods of lactational amenorrhea, on postmenopausal bone mass. The effect of frequent lactational amenorrhea on bone mass needs to be investigated. Research efforts to understand the role of estrogen in the etiology of osteoporosis have been limited to samples in industrialized societies who rarely experience frequent childbearing and long periods of lactational amenorrhea. Cross-cultural studies addressing the above-mentioned issues will contribute new insights into the study of menopause, and the etiology of osteoporosis.

Appendix:

A Comparison of the Distribution of Fertility Patterns For Mayan and Greek Women

Table A
Marital Status of Women in Chichimila (N=107)

	N	%
Married	93	87
Divorced	1	.9
Separated	3	2.8
Widowed	4	3.7
Single	5	4.7
Living Together	1	.9

Table B
Marital Status of Women in Stira (N = 96)

	N	%
Married	92	95.8
Widowed	3	3.1
Single	1	1.1
Divorced	0	0
Separated	0	0
Cohabiting	0	0

Table C
Comparison of Age at Birth of First Child

	Mayan (N = 100)		Greek (N = 88)	
Age at Birth of First Child	N	Percent	N	Percent
14	2	2.0	—	—
15	7	7.0	—	—
16	11	11.0	1	1.0
17	9	9.0	—	—
18	10	10.0	2	2.3
19	15	15.0	4	4.5
20	9	9.0	6	6.8
21	8	8.0	4	4.5
22	7	7.0	6	6.8
23	5	5.0	7	8.0
24	3	3.0	11	12.5
25	4	4.0	4	4.5
26-35	10	10.0	38	43.0
36 and older	—	—	5	5.6
Total	100	100	88	100

Table D
Comparison of the Distribution of Pregnancies
for Mayan and Greek Women

	Mayan Woman (N = 100)		Greek Woman (N = 88)	
Number of Pregnancies	N = 104	Percent	N = 95	Percent
0	2	1.9	4	4.2
1	7	6.7	5	5.3
2	3	2.9	37	38.9
3	7	6.7	29	30.5
4	9	8.7	8	8.4
5	8	7.7	4	4.2
6	12	11.5	5	5.3
7	13	12.5	2	2.1
8	9	8.7	—	—
9	7	6.7	—	—
10 and more	27	25.9	1	1.1
Total	104	100	95	100

Table E
Comparison of the Distribution of Number of Living Offspring
for Mayan and Greek Women

	Mayan (N = 102)		Greek (N = 91)	
Number of Living Offspring	N	Percent	N	Percent
0	3	2.9	3	3.3
1	12	11.8	7	7.7
2	7	6.9	48	52.7
3	14	13.7	22	24.2
4	15	14.7	6	6.6
5	11	10.8	2	2.2
6	10	9.8	2	2.2
7	12	11.8	—	—
8	11	10.8	1	1.1
9	3	2.9	—	—
10	3	2.9	—	—
11	1	1.0	—	—
Total	102	100	91	100

Table F
Comparison of the Distribution of Child Mortality
for Mayan and Greek Women

	Mayan Women (N = 101)		Greek Women (N = 89)	
Child Mortality	N = 101	Percent	N = 89	Percent
0	46	45.5	82	92.1
1	27	26.7	7	7.9
2	11	10.9	—	—
3	10	9.9	—	—
4	3	3.0	—	—
5	3	3.0	—	—
6	1	1.0	—	—
Total	101	100	89	100

Bibliography

Achte, K.
  1970   "Menopause from the Psychiatrist's Point of View." *Acta Obstetrica et Gynecologica Scandanavica* 1 (supplement): 3–17.

Akesode, A., Migeon, J., and Kowarski, A.
  1977   "Effect of Food Intake on the Metabolic Clearance Rate of Aldosterone." *Journal of Clincial Endocrinology and Metabolism* 45:849.

Aloia, J. F. et al.,
  1983   "Determinants of Bone Mass in Postmenopausal Women." *Arch Internal Medicine* 143:1700–4.

Ardener, S.
  1975   *Perceiving Women.* New York: John Wiley & Sons.

Atkinson, P. J. and West, R. R.
  1970   "Loss of Skeletal Calcium in Lactating Women." *Journal of Obstet Gynecol Br. Commonwealth* 77:555–60.

Bachman, G.
  1984   "Evaluation of the Climacteric Women—An Overview. *Midpoint,* vol. 1 (1):9–13.

Balam, G.
  1981   *La Migracion en el Area de los Centros Coordinadores del I.N.I. de Yucatan: El Bracerismo Regional y sus Repercusiones Sociales.* Valladolid, Yucatan.

145

Ballinger, C. B.
   1975   "Psychiatric Morbidity and the Menopause: Screening of a General
           Population Sample." *British Medical Journal* 3(5979) August:344–346.

   1976   "Psychiatric Morbidity and the Menopause: Clinical Features." *British
           Medical Journal* 1(6019) May:1183–85.

   1977   "Psychiatric Morbidity and the Menopause: Survey of a Gynecologi-
           cal Out-Patient Clinic." *British Journal of Psychiatry* 131(July:83–89.

Barr, W.
   1975   "Problems Related to Postmenopausal Women." *South African
           Medical Journal* 49(March):437–39.

Bart, P.
   1971   "Depression in Middle-Aged Women." In *Women in the Sexist
           Society.* V. Gornick and B. Moran (eds.), New York: Basic Books.

Benedek, T.
   1950   "Climacterium: A Developmental Phase." *Psychoanalitic Quarterly*
           19:1–27.

Blum, R. and Blum, E.
   1965   *Health and Healing in Rural Greece: A Study of Three Communities.*
           Stanford: Stanford University Press.

Bohler, C. S. and Greenblatt, R.
   1974   "The Pathophysiology of the Hot Flush." In *The Menopausal Syn-
           drome,* pp. 29–37. Edited by R. B. Greenblatt, V. B. Mahesh, and
           P. G. McDonough. New York: Medcom Press.

Brody, J.
   1979   "Menopausal Estrogens: Benefits and Risks of the 'Feminine' Drug."
           Forum 2 (Fall):10–11.

Brown, J. and Brown, M.
   1976   "Psychiatric Disorders Associated with the Menopause." In *The
           Menopause: A Guide to Current Research and Practices,* pp. 57–59.
           Edited by Robert Beard, Baltimore: University Park Press.

Brown, M.
   1976   "Emotional Response to the Menopause." In *The Management of the
           Menopause and Post-Menopausal Years,* pp. 109–15. Edited by Stuart
           Campbell. Lancaster, England: MTP Press, Ltd.

Bungay, G., Vessay, M., and McPherson, C.
   1980   "Study of Symptoms in Middle Life with Special Reference to
           Menopause." *British Medical Journal* 281:181–83.

Cabrera, L.
1980   *Plantas Curativas de Mexico.* Mexico 1, D. F.: LibroMex Editores, S. de R.L.

Campbell, J.
1964   *Honour, Family and Patronage. Oxford:* Clarendon Press.

Carroll, J.
1983   "Middle Age Does Not Mean Menopause." *Topics in Clinical Nursing.* January:38–44.

Chavez, A. and Rosado, A. P.
1967   "Estudio Epidemiologico de la Pelagra en Una Communidad Rural." *Boletin del Oficina Sanitaria Panamericana* 55(4):398–404.

Chowdhury, N.
1969   "Menopause and Its Problems." *Journal of the Indian Medical Association* 53(July):16–17.

Clark, M.
1967   "The Anthropology of Aging, A New Area of Studies of Culture and Personality." *The Gerontologist* 7: 55–64.

Cole, P., Brown, J., and MacMahon, B.
1976   "Estrogen Profiles of Parous and Nulliparous Women." *The Lancet* (September 18): 596–99.

Cooper, W.
1976   "A Woman's View of the Menopause." In *The Management of the Menopause and Post-Menopausal Years,* pp. 3–9. Edited by Stuart Campbell. Lancaster, England: MTP Press, Ltd.

Cravioto, R. et al.
1945   "Nutritive Value of the Tortilla." *Science* 102:91–93.

Crawford, M. and Hooper, D.
1973   "Menopause, Aging and the Family." *Social Science and Medicine* 7(June):469–82.

Daniell, H. W.
1976   "Osteoporosis of the Slender Smoker: Vertebral Compression Fractures and Loss of Metacarpal Cortex in Relation to Postmenopausal Cigarette Smoking and Lack of Obesity." *Arch Internal Medicine* 136:298–304.

Davila, M.
1971   "Compadrazgo: Fictive Kinship in Latin America." In *Readings in Kinship and Social Structure,* pp. 396–406. Edited by N. Graburn. New York: Harper & Row.

Davis, D. L.
1982   "Women's Status and Experience of the Menopause In Newfoundland Fishing Village." *Maturitas* 4:207–16.

Dennerstein, L. and Burrows, G.
1978   "A Review of Studies of the Psychological Symptoms Found at Menopause." *Maturitas* 1:55–64.

Deutsch, H.
1945   *The Psychology of Women.* New York: Grune & Stratton.

Diaz-Bolio, J.
1981   "El Mal de Huesos y La Chaya." *Diario de Yucatan,* (16 de Septiembre), Merida, Yucatan.

Dominian, J.
1977   "The Role of Psychiatry in the Menopause." *Clinical Obstetrics and Gynecology* 4 (April):241–58.

Dougherty, M.
1978   "An Anthropological Perspective on Aging and Women in the Middle Years." In *The Anthropology of Health,* pp. 167–76. Edited by Eleanor Bauwens. St. Louis: Mosby.

Douglas, M.
1966   *Purity and Danger: An Analysis of Concepts of Pollution and Taboo.* London: Routledge & Kegan Paul.

Dowty, N., et al.
1970   "Climacterium in Three Cultural Contexts." *Tropical and Geographical Medicine* 22:77–86.

DuBoulay, J.
1974   *Portrait of Greek Mountain Village.* Oxford: Clarendon Press.

Ehrenreich, B. and English, D.
1973   *Complaints and Disorders. The Sexual Politics of Sickness.* New York: The Feminist Press.

Ehrenreich, B. and Ehrenreich, J.
1970   *The American Health Empire: Power, Profits, and Politics.* New York: Vintage Books.

Elmendorf, M.
1976   *Nine Mayan Women, A Village Faces Change.* New York: Schenkman Publishing, Inc.

Engel, G.
1962   *Psychological Development in Health and Disease.* Philadelphia: W. B. Saunders and Co.

Eveleth, P. and Tanner, J.
1976   *World Wide Variation in Human Growth.* Cambridge: Cambridge University Press.

Feeley, E. and Pyne, H.
1975   "The Menopause: Facts and Misconceptions." *Nursing Forum* 14:74–86.

Fessler, L.
1950   "Psychopathology of Climacteric Depression." *Psychoanalytic Quarterly* 19:28–42.

Flint, M.
1979   "The Sociology and Anthropology of Menopause." In *Female and Male Climacteric, Current Opinion,* pp. 1–8. Edited by Peter van Keep, D. Serr, and R. Greenblatt. Baltimore: University Park Press.

1976   "Cross-Cultural Factors That Affect the Age of Menopause." In *Consensus on Menopause Research,* pp. 73–83. Edited by Peter van Keep, R. Greenblatt and M. Albeaux-Fernet. Baltimore: University Park Press.

1975   "The Menopause: Reward or Punishment?" *Psychosomatics* 16 (Winter):161–163.

Foster, G. and Anderson, B.
1978   *Medical Anthropology.* New York: John Wiley & Sons.

Foster, G.
1961   "The Dyadic Contract: A Model for the Social Structure of a Mexican Peasant Village." *American Anthropologist* 63:1173–92.

Frey, K. A.
1981   "Middle-Aged Women's Experience and Perceptions of Menopause." *Women & Health* (1/2):25–36.

Friederich, M.
1982   "Aging, Menopause, and Estrogen: The Clinician's Dilemma." In *Changing Perspectives on Menopause,* pp. 336–45. Edited by A. Voda, M. Dinnerstein, and S. O'Donnell. Austin: University of Texas Press.

Friedl, E.
1962   *Vasilika: A Village in Modern Greece.* New York: Holt, Rinehart and Winston.

Frisch, R.
1980   "Fatness, Puberty and Fertility." *Natural History* 89:16–27.

Frisch, R. and McArthur, J.
1974 "Menstrual Cycles: Fatness as a Determinant of Minimum Weight for Height Necessary for Their Maintenance or Onset." *Science* 185:949–50.

Furuhjelm, M. and Fedor-Freybergh, P.
1976 "The Influence of Estrogens on the Psyche in Climacteric and Post-Menopausal Women." In *Consensus on Menopause Research,* pp. 84–94. Edited by P. van Keep, R. Greenblatt, and M. Albeaux-Fernet. Baltimore: University Park Press.

Garn, S. M.
1970 *The Earlier Gains and Later Loss of Cortical Bone.* Springfield, Ill.: Charles C. Thomas Publishing Inc.

Garn, S. M., Rohnann, C. G., and Wagner, B.
1976 "Bone Loss as a General Phenomenon in Man." *Fed. Proc.* 26 (6):1729–36.

Genant, H. K., et al.
1982 "Quantitative Computed Tomography of Vertebral Spongiosa: A Sensitive Method for Detecting Early Bone Loss After Oophorectomy." *Annals of Internal Medicine* 97:699–705.

Goodman, M.
1982 "A Critique of Menopause Research." In *Changing Perspective on Menopause,* pp. 273–88. Edited by A. Voda, M. Dinnerstein, and S. O'Donnell. Austin: University of Texas Press.

1980 "Toward a Biology of Menopause." *Signs: A Journal of Women in Culture and Society* 5 (4):740–53.

Goodman, M., Stewart, C., and Gilbert, F.
1977 "Patterns of Menopause: A Study of Certain Medical and Physiological Variables Among Caucasian and Japanese Women Living in Hawaii." *Journal of Gerontology* 32:291–98.

Greene, J.
1983 "Bereavement and Social Support at the Climacteric." *Maturitas* 5:115–124.

Greene, J. and Cooke, D.
1980 "Life Stress and Symptoms at the Climacteric." *British Journal of Psychiatry* 136:486–91.

Greenblatt, R. and Bruneteau, D.
1974 "Menopausal Headaches: Psychogenic or Metabolic?" *Journal of American Geriatric Society* 22(April):291–98.

Griffen, J.
1982 "Cultural Models for Coping with Menopause." In *Changing Perspective on Menopause*, pp. 248–62. Edited by A. Voda, M. Dinnerstein, and S. O'Donnell. Austin: University of Texas Press.

1977 "A Cross-Cultural Investigation of Behavioral Changes at Menopause." *A Social Science Journal* (April) vol. 14, No. 2:49–55.

Harwood, A.
1971 "The Hot-Cold Theory of Disease: Implications for Treatment of Puerto Rican Patients." *The Journal of the American Medical Association* 216:1153–58.

Heath, D.
1979 *El Libro del Judio o Medicina Domestica.* Merida, Yucatan, Mexico.

Hill, P., et al.
1976 "Plasma Hormone Levels in Different Ethnic Populations of Women." *Cancer Research* (July) 36: 2297–301.

Hill, P., et al.
1977 "Diet and Endocrine-Related Cancer." *Cancer* 39:1820–26.

Hill, P., et al.
1980 "Diet, Lifestyle, and Menstrual Activity." *The American Journal of Clinical Nutrition* (June)33:1192–98.

Hirschon, R.
1978 "Open Body/Closed Space: The Transformation of Female Sexuality." In *Defining Females: The Nature of Women in Society*, pp. 66–88. Edited by S. Ardener. New York: John Wiley & Sons.

Holte, A. and Mikkelsen, A.
1982 "Menstrual Coping Style, Social Background and Climacteric Symptoms." *Psychiatry and Social Science* 2:41–45.

Hoskins, R.
1944 "Psychological Treatment of the Menopause." *Journal of Clinical Endocrinology* 4:605–10.

Hurd, H., Palumbo, J. and Gharib, H.
1977 "Hypothalamic Endocrine Dysfunction in Anorexia Nervosa." *Mayo Clinic Proceedings* 52:711–16.

Jordan, B.
1981 *Birth in Four Cultures: A Cross-Cultural Investigation of Childbirth in Yucatan, Holland, Sweden and the United States.* Third Edition. Montreal: Eden Press.

Kacyaski, J. S. and Anderson, K. L.
  1974   "Age Dependent Osteoporosis Among Men Habituated to a High-Level of Physical Activity." *Acta Morpho Neerl Scan* 12:283–92.

Kaufert, P.
  1982   "Myth and The Menopause." *Sociology of Health and Illness* 4(2):141–66.

Kaufert, P. and Gilbert, P.
  1986   "Women, Menopause and Medicalization." *Culture, Medicine and Psychiatry* 10 (3):7–22.

Kaufert, P. and Syrotuik, J.
  1981   "Symptom Reporting at Menopause." *Social Science and Medicine* 15:173–84.

Koninckx, P.
  1984   "Menopause: The Beginning of a Curable Disease or a Lucky Phenomenon." In *The Climacteric: An Update.* Edited by H. and B. van Herendael, F. E. Riphagen, L. Goessens and H. van der Pas. Lancaster: MTP Press Limited.

Konner, M. and Worthman, C.
  1980   "Nursing Frequency, Gonadal Function, and Birth Spacing among !Kung Hunters-Gatherers." *Science* 207:788–91.

Kopera, H.
  1978   "Effects, Side-Effects, and Dosage Schemes of Various Sex Hormones in the Peri- and Post-Menopause." Workshop Report in *Female and Male Climacteric,* pp. 43–67. Edited by P. van Keep, D. Serr, and R. Greenblatt. Baltimore: University Park Press.

Kuoppasalmi, K., et al.
  1976   "Effect of Strenuous Anaerobic Running Exercise on Plasma Growth Hormone, Cortisol, Luteinizing Hormone, Testosterone, Androstenedione, Estrone and Estradiol." *Journal of Steroid Biochem* 7 (10):823–29.

LaRocco, S. A. and Polit, D. F.
  1980   "Women's Knowledge about the Menopause." *Nursing Research* 29:10-13.

Landa, D. F.
  1978   *Yucatan: Before and After the Conquest.* Translated by William Gates. Toronto: General Publishing Company, Ltd.

Lauritzen, C.
  1976   "The Estrogen Deficiency Syndrome and the Management of the Patient." In *Consensus on Menopause Research,* pp. 37–43. Edited

by P. van Keep, R. Greenblatt, and M. Albeaux-Fernet. Baltimore: University Park Press.

1976   "The Female Climacteric Syndrome: Significance, Problems, Treatment." *Acta Obstetrica et Gynecologica Scandanavica* 51 (supplement):49–60.

Leiblum, S. R. and Swartzman, L. C.
1986   "Women's Attitudes Toward the Menopause: An Update." *Maturitas* 8:47–56.

Lennane, K. and Lennane, R.
1973   "Alleged Psychogenic Disorder in Women: A Possible Manifestation of Sexual Prejudice." *New England Journal of Medicine* 288:288.

Lindsay, R.
1984   "The Role of Estrogen in the Development of Osteoporosis." *In Proceedings of the National Institutes of Health Consensus Development Conference*, 59–61, April 2–4.

Lindsay, R. et al.
1980   "Prevention of Spinal Osteoporosis in Oophorectomised Women." *Lacent* 2:1151–53.

Lock, M.
1982   "Models and Practice in Medicine: Menopause as Syndrome or Life Transition?" *Culture, Medicine, and Psychiatry* 6:261–80.

Logan, M.
1973   "Humoral Medicine in Guatemala and Peasant Acceptance of Modern Medicine." *Human Organization* 32:385–95.

MacMahon, B. and Cole, P.
1971   "Estrogen Profiles of Asian and North American Women." *The Lancet*, (October 23): 900–902.

MacMahon, B., et al.
1974   "Urine Estrogen Profiles of Asian and North American Women." *International Journal of Cancer* 14:161–167.

MacPherson, K.
1981   "Menopause as Disease: The Social Construction of a Metaphor." *Advances in Nursing Science* 3(2):95–113.

McCrea, F.
1983   "The Politics of Menopause: The Discovery of Deficiency Disease." *Social Problems* (October) 13(1):111–23.

McCullough, J.
1973   "Human Ecology, Heat Adaptation, and Belief Systems: The Hot-Cold Syndrome of Yucatan." *Journal of Anthropological Research* 29:32–36.

McKinlay, S. and McKinlay, J.
1985 "Health Status and Health Care Utilization by Menopausal Women." In *Aging Reproduction and the Climacteric.* Edited by L. Mastroianni and C. Paulson. New York: Plenum.

McKinlay, S. and Jeffery, M.
1974 "The Menopause Syndrome." *British Journal of Medicine* 28:108–15.

McNall, S. G.
1974 *The Greek Peasant.* Washington, D. C.: American Sociological Association.

McNatty, K. P., Sawers, R. S., and McNeilly, A. S.
1979 "A Possible Role for Prolactin in Control of Steroid Secretion by Human Graafian Follicle." *Nature* 250:653–55.

McNeilly, A. S.
1979 "Effects of Lactation on Fertility." *British Medical Bulletin* 35:151–54.

Madden, J. D., et al.
1978 "Analysis of Secretory Patterns of Prolactin and Gonadotropins During Twenty-Four Hours in a Lactating Woman Before and After Resumption of Menses." *American Journal of Obstetrics and Gynecology* 132 (4):436–41.

Maffia, L.
1974 "Protein Quality of Two Varieties of High Lysine Maize Fed Alone and with Black Beans or Milk in Normal and Depleted Weanling Rats." *Western Hemisphere Nutrition Congress IV* August 19–22, p. 72.

Mamdani, M.
1973 *The Myth of Population Control: Family, Caste, and Class in an Indian Village.* New York: Monthly Review Press.

Maoz, B. et al.
1977 "The Perception of Menopause in Five Ethnic Groups in Israel." *Acta Obstetrica et Gynecologica Scandanavica* 65 (supplement):35–40.

Maoz, B. et al.
1970 "Female Attitudes to Menopause." *Social Psychiatry* 5: 35–40.

Martin, C. M. and Hoffman, P. G.
1983 "The Endocrinology of Pregnancy." In *Basic and Clinical Endocrinology,* pp. 456–78. Edited by F. S. Greenspan and P. H. Forsham. Los Altos: Lange Medical Publications.

May, M. J.
1963 The Ecology of Malnutrition in Five Countries of Eastern and Central Europe. New York: Hafner Publishing Company.

May, M. J. and Donna, L.
   1972   *The Ecology of Malnutrition in Mexico and Central America*. New
          York: Hafner Publishing Ccompany.

Merimee, T. and Fineberge, S.
   1974   "Growth Hormone Secretion in Starvation—A Reassessment." *Jour-
          nal of Clinical Endocrinology and Metabolism* 39:385–86.

Mikkelsen, A. and Holte, A.
   1982   "A Factor-Analytic Study of Climacteric Symptoms." *Psychiatry and
          Social Science* 2:35–39.

Moloney, J.
   1975   "Systematic Valence Coding of Mexican 'Hot'-'Cold' Foods." *Ecology
          of Food and Nutrition* 4:67–74.

Murdock, G.
   1963   *Outline of World Cultures*. Third edition. New Haven: Human
          Relations Area Files, Inc.

Murguia, R.
   1979   "La Milpa y Los Milperos." *Yucatan: Historia y Econmia*, Ano 2, No.
          10-11-12 (November 1978–April 1979):21–43. Departamento de
          Estudios Economicos y Sociales Centro de Investigaciones Regionales,
          Universidad de Yucatan.

Nash, J.
   1970   *In the Eyes of the Ancestors: Belief and Behavior in a Maya Com-
          munity*. New Haven: Yale University Press.

National Institutes of Health
   1979   *Estrogen Use and Postmenopausal Women. National Institutes of
          Health Consensus Development Conference Summary*. Vol. 2, No. 8.

Navidades
   1981   "Un Policia Muerto Y Siete Heridos Ayer al Volcar el Vehiculo del
          Grupo Antimotines." Septiembre 28, Merida Yucatan.

Neugarten, B. and Kraines, R.
   1965   "Menopausal Symptoms in Women of Various Ages." *Psychosomatic
          Medicine* 27:266–73.

Neugarten, B. et al.
   1968   "Women's Attitudes toward the Menopause." In *Middle Age and
          Aging*, pp. 195–200. Edited by B. Neugarten. Chicago: The Univer-
          sity of Chicago Press.

Neville, C. M.
1983 "Regulation of Mammary Development and Lactation." In Lactation: *Physiological, Nutritional and Breast-Feeding.* Edited by M. C. Neville and M. R. Neifert. New York: Plenum Press.

Nordin, C.
1982 "Bone Loss at the Menopause." *Menopause Update,* vol. 1(1):5-9.

1966 "International Patterns of Osteoporosis." *Clinical Orthopaedic and Related Research* 45:17-30.

Notelovitz, M.
1978 "The Menopause and Its Treatment." *Journal of the Florida Medical Association* 65(May):34-44.

Page, J.
1977 *The Other Awkward Age: Menopause.* Berkeley: Ten Speed Press.

Parlee, M.
1976 "Social Factors in the Psychology of Menstruation, Birth, and Menopause." *Primary Care* 3 (September):477-90.

Pelto, P. and Pelto, G.
1978 *Anthropological Research. The Structure of Inquiry.* Second edition. Cambridge: Cambridge University Press.

Peter, H.
1978 "The Aging Ovary." Workshop Report in *Female and Male Climacteric,* pp. 17-21. Edited by P. van Keep, D. Serr, and R. Greenblatt. Baltimore: University Park Press.

Peterson, A. and Taylor, B.
1980 "The Biological Approach to Adolescence." In *Handbook of Adolescent Psychology,* pp.117-55. Edited by J. Adelson. New York: John Wiley & Sons, Inc.

Posner, J.
1979 "It's All in Your Head: Feminist and Medical Models of Menopause (Strange Bedfellows)." *Sex Roles* vol. 5, no. 2:179-90.

Prados, M.
1967 "Emotional Factors in the Climacterium of Women." *Psychotherapy Psychosomatic* 15:231-44.

Press, I.
1975 *Tradition and Adaptation: Life in a Modern Yucatan Maya Village.* Westport: Greenwood Press.

Redfield, R.
1941 *The Folk Culture of Yucatan.* Chicago: The University of Chicago Press.

Redfield, R. and Villa Rojas, A.
1934 *Chan Kom A Maya Village.* Chicago: The University of Chicago Press.

Reed, N.
1964 *The Caste War of Yucatan.* Stanford: Stanford University Press.

Reitz, R.
1977 *Menopause: A Positive Approach.* New York: Penguin Books.

Richelson, L. S. et al.
1984 "Relative Contribution of Aging and Estrogen Deficiency to Postmenopausal Bone Loss." *New England Journal of Medicine* 311:1273–75.

Rosenzweig, S.
1943 "Psychology of the Menstrual Cycle." *Journal of Clinical Endocrinology* 3: 296–300.

Ross, M.
1951 "Psychosomatic Approach to the Climacterium." *California Medicine* 74:240–42.

Rothman, B.
1979 "Women, Health and Medicine." In *Women: A Feminist Perspective,* pp. 27–40. Edited by J. Freeman. Palo Alto: Mayfield Publishing Co.

Schneider, H.
1979 "Sociology and Anthropology of Menopause." In *Female and Male Climacteric, Current Opinion,* pp. 1–8. Edited by P. van Keep, D. Serr, and R. Greenblatt. Baltimore: University Park Press.

Schneider, M. and Brotherton, P.
1979 "Physiological, Psychological and Situational Stressess in Depression During the Climacteric." *Maturitas* 1:153–58.

Scully, D.
1980 *Men who Control Women's Health: The Miseducation of Obstetrician-Gynecologists.* Boston: Houghton-Mifflin Company.

Seaman, B. and Seaman, G.
1977 *Women and the Crisis in Sex Hormones.* New York: Rawson Associates Publishers, Inc.

Severne, L.
1979 "Psycho-Social Aspect of the Menopause." In *Psychosomatic in Peri-Menopause.* Edited by A. Haspels and H. Musaph. Lancaster: MTP Press.

Seylwyn, C.
   1977   "Hot Flushes and Cold Turkey." *British Medical Journal* 1 (June
          18):1599.

Shattuck, G.
   1933   *The Peninsula of Yucatan.* Published by the Carnegie Institution of
          Washington, Washington, D. C.

Short, R. V.
   1978   "Healthy Infertility." *Upsala Journal of Medical Science* Suppl.
          22:23–26.

Simpson-Herbert, M. and Huffman, S. L.
   1981   "The Contraceptive Effect of Breast-Feeding." *Studies in Family Plan-
          ning* 12:125–33.

Skultans, V.
   1970   "The Symbolic Significance of Menstruation and Menopause." *Man*
          vol. 5(4):639–51.

Smith, R. W.
   1967   "Dietary and Hormonal Factors in Bone Loss." *Fed Proc.* 26:1736–47.

Snowden, R. and Christian, B.
   1983   *Patterns and Perceptions of Menstruation.* New York: St. Martin's
          Press.

Spencer, R. P., Sagel, S. S., and Garn, S. M.
   1968   "Age Change in Five Parameters of Metacarpal Growth." *Inv.
          Radiology* 3:27–34.

Spradley, J.
   1980   *Participant Observation.* New York: Holt, Rinehart and Winston.

   1979   *The Ethnographic Interview.* New York: Holt, Rinehart and Winston.

Stadel, B. and Weiss, N.
   1975   "Characteristics of Menopausal Women: A Survey of King and Pierce
          Counties in Washington, 1973–1974." *American Journal of
          Epidemiology* 102:209–16.

Steggerda, M.
   1941   *Maya Indians of Yucatan.* Washington, D. C.: Carnegie Publication
          No. 531.

Tanner, J.
   1978   *Foetus into Man.* Cambridge, Mass.: Harvard University Press.

Thijssen, J. and Longcope, C.
   1976   "Post-Menopausal Estrogen Production." Workshop Report in *Consensus on Menopause Research*, pp. 25–28. Edited by P. van Keep, R. Greenblatt, and M. Albeaux-Fernet. Baltimore: University Park Press.

Thompson, R.
   1974   *The Winds of Tomorrow: Social Change in a Maya Town*. Chicago: The University of Chicago Press.

Townsend, J. and Carbone, C.
   1980   "Menopausal Syndrome: Illness or Social Role—A Transcultural Analysis." *Culture, Medicine and Psychiatry* 4:229–48.

Uphold, C. and Susman, E.
   1981   "Self-Reported Climacteric Symptoms as Function of the Relationship Between Marital Adjustment and Child Rearing Stages." *Nursing Research* 30:84–88..

U. S. Department of Health, Education and Welfare, Public Health Service.
   1966   *Age at Menopause, United States 1960–1962. Vital Health Statistics. Data from National Health Survey*. Public Health Service Publication No. 1000. Series 11. No. 19. Washington, D. C.: U. S. Government Printing Office.

   1979   *The Older Women: Continuities and Discontinuities*. NIH Publication No. 79–1897. Washington, D..C.: U. S. Government Printing Office.

   1959   *Menopause Health Information Series*. Publication No. 179. Washington, D. C.: U. S. Government Printing Office.

Utian, W. H.
   1980   *Menopause in Modern Prespective. Guide to Clinical Practice*. New York: Appleton Century Crofts.

   1976   "The Scientific Basis for Post-menopausal Estrogen Therapy: The Management of Specific Symptoms and Rationale for Long-Term Replacement." In *The Menopause*, pp. 175–201. Edited by R. Beard. Baltimore: University Park Press.

Utian, W. and Serr, D.
   1976   "The Climacteric Syndrome." In *Consensus on Menopause Research*, pp.1–4. Edited by P. van Keep, R. Greenblatt, and M. Albeaux-Fernet. Baltimore: University Park Press.

van Keep, P. and Humphrey, M.
   1976   "Psycho-Social Aspects of Climacteric." In *Consensus on Menopause Research*, pp. 5–8. Edited by P. van Keep, R. Greenblatt, and M. Albeaux-Fernet. Baltimore: University Park Press.

van Keep, P., and Kellerhals, J.
1974 "The Impact of Socio-Cultural Factors on Symptom Formation." *Psychotherapy Psychosomatic* 231:251–63.

1976 "The Aging Women: About the Influence of Some Social and Cultural Factors on the Changes in Attitude and Behavior that Occur during and after the Menopause." *Acta Obstetrica et Gynecologica Scandanavica* 51 (supplement):17–27.

van Keep, P., Serr, D., and Greenblatt, R., eds.
1979 *Female and Male Climacteric, Current Opinion.* Baltimore: University Park Press.

Voda, A. and Eliasson, M.
1983 "Menopause: The Closure of Menstrual Life." In *Lifting the Curse of Menstruation,* pp. 137–56. Edited by S. Golub. New York: The Haworth Press.

Voda, A., Dinnerstein, M., and O'Donnell, S. eds.
1982 *Changing Perspectives on Menopause.* Austin: University of Texas Press.

Vogt, E.
1969 *Zinacantan: A Maya Community in the Highlands of Chiapas.* Cambridge, Mass.: The Belknap Press of Harvard University Press.

Wardlaw, G. M. and Pike, A. M.
1986 "The Effect of Lactation on Peak Adult Shaft and Ultradistal Forearm Bone Mass in Women." *American Journal of Clinical Nutrition* 44(August):283–86.

Wentz, A.
1976 "Psychiatric Morbidity and the Menopause." *Annal of Internal Medicine* 84(March):331–33.

Whitlock, R.
1976 *Everyday Life of the Maya.* New York: G. P. Putnam and Sons.

Wilson, R.
1966 *Feminine Forever.* New York: M. Evans and Co.

Wilson, R. and Wilson, T.
1963 "The Fate of the Non-Treated Postmenopausal Women: A Plea for the Maintenance of Adequate Estrogen from Puberty to the Grave." *Journal of the American Geriatric Society* 11:347–62.

Winokur, G.
1973 "Depression in the Menopause." *American Journal of Psychiatry* 130 (January):92–93.

Wood, C.
  1979   "Menopausal Myths." *Medical Journal of Australia* 1:496–99.

World Bank
  1981   *Accelerated Development in Sub-Saharan Africa: An Agenda for Action.* Table 34, pp. 177, Washington, D. C.

World Health Organization
  1977   *The Ninth Revision of the International Classification of Diseases.* London: HMSO.

Wyshak, G.
  1981   "Hip Fracture in Elderly Women and Reproductive History." *Journal of Gerontology* 36:424–27.

Index

Abortion: as a birth control method, in rural Greece, 113; as a moral issue, 114; as a source of gossip, 113. See also birth control; contraceptives.

Acculturation among Mayans, 31. See also Catrin

Adulthood in Mayan culture, 84

Aged parents, care of, in rural Greece, 56, 101

Ageism, in Western culture, 16, 23

Aging: attitudes toward, 22, 15; Greeks, 56, 101, 130; and menopause, 18; and status, 130; anxiety of, 114; of the ovaries, 12

Agriculture: terracing, 53; slash and burn, 33, 34, 36, 40; cycle of, in Greece, 53; in Yucatan, 34. See also farming

Alcohol: consumption of, in rural Mayan villages, 85; as a social event, 87

Alcoholism: among Mayan men, 86; and wife abuse, 86; as causes of distress, 86; and migration to Can Cun, 86–87; in rural Greece, 102

Amenorrhea: postpartum, 137; and lactation, 111, 136

Anemia: condition of, among Mayan women, 132; nutritional, 135; and childbearing, 122

Anxiety: and menopause, 12, 14, 15, 126, 129, 130; of aging, 114; freedom from, 129; of unwanted pregnancy, 124; among Mayan women, 88. See also menopause; pregnancy

Atole, defined, 82. See also food; maize

Authority, hierarchy of, in Mayan culture, 73

Birth, management of, in Mayan culture, 112; in rural Greece, 114

Birth Control: abortion, 113; attitudes toward, 88; use of, 113, 132; and fear of sterility, 108; lack of, among Mayan women, 88. See also abortion; contraceptives

Blood, cleansing of, 126. See also menstruation

Bochorno, defined, 118, 119, 122

Breast-feeding, 137; length of, 132. See also lactation

Bone, fracture, see osteoporosis

Calcium: in take of, 136; depletion of, 13; and lactation, 138. See also osteoporosis

Cast War, 36, 37

Catrins, definition of, 31; criteria of being, 32-33

Chaya, 82. See also vegetables

Childbearing: 132; decision of, in Mayan household, 80; patterns of, 139; stress of, 130; comparison of, Greek and Mayan women, 129. See also fertility

Childhood, in Mayan culture, 80, 84

Children: attitudes toward, 109; responsibilities of, to their deceased parents, 110; importance of, 110, 112; as security for old age, 109, 113

Cleanliness, value of, 64, 83. See also hygiene

Climacteric, definition of, 11

Clothing: regional, in rural Greece, 52; and marital status, and age, 53; Maya, 32

Compadrazgo, see fictive kin; godparents

Contraceptive: oral, fear of, 108; use of, 113; lack of, 111, 116. See also birth control

Corn, consumption of, 135. See also agriculture; diet; farming

Curandero, 43, 44, 45. See also healers

Dengue, 48

Descent, 38. See also kinship

Depression, 12, 14-15, 20. See also symptoms

Diet: 131-132, 139; of Mayan villagers, 82, 117, 110, 132; of Mexicans, 135; of rural Greeks, 98-99; and ecology, 132; and hormone production, 133; and menstrual cycle, 133; and pituitary activity, 133, 134; and physical development, 133

Disease: definition of, in rural Greece, 59; classification of, into hot and cold, 41; paradigm of, 12; symptoms of, 125; infectious, 48

Disease model: 16-18, 115; of menopause, 18-19; feminist view of, 19

Disputes, cause of, among Mayan women, and settling of, 85

Divination, in rural Greece, 59, 61, 63

Divorce, 84. See also women

Dowry, 96, 101

Education: among Mayan villagers, 31-32; value of, in rural Greece, 55, 96; barrier of, for girls, 96-97; cost of, 55-56, 101; impact of, on fertility, 112; and urban migration, 55

Ejido, 33, 36, 87, 135. See also landownership

Election, political, in Mayan village, 37; Greek, 57

Emigration: in Greek villages, 70; causes of, 101. See also education

Empty nest, syndrome of, at menopause, 15, 20, 21

Endometrium Carcinoma, 138. See also estrogen

Estrogen: decrease of, and metabolic changes, 14; deficiency syndrome of, 13; deficiency of, at menopause, 12, 137; and hot flashes, 123; levels of, during lactation, 137; production of, and the ovaries, 13; theraputic use of, 17, 18; and conference about 23; stimulation of, and breast cancer, 138; and endometrium carcinoma, 138; 131; and osteoporosis, 139

Ethiopia, 62, 69, 71

Ethnography, aim of, 4-5; methods of, 5-7

Evil eye: definition of, 45, 61; symptoms of, 61; and treatment of, 61-62. See also illness

Family: network of, 37–39, 57–58;
nuclear, as an economic unit, 57; size
of, Mayan, 109; Greek, 112; responsibilities of, in Greek household, 100;
to decrease members, Mayan, 110;
honor of, 96
Family planning: decision of, 114;
attitudes toward, 108–109. See also
birth control; contraceptives
Farming: techniques of, 70, 132, 134.
See also agriculture
Fat, intake of, and hormone production, 133. See also diet; estrogen
Father: roles of, 97; as disciplinary
figure, 97
Fecundity: 3, 110, 133; importance of,
108, 121. See also fertility
Female roles: 89, 129; apprenticeship in,
68–69, 72. See also roles; women
Femininity, loss of, and menopause,
14–15, 19
Fertility: patterns of, 131–132, 136; and
bone density, 137; and reproductive
system, 139; loss of, at menopause,
120. See also fecundity
Fictive kin: in Latin America 37, 38,
39; in Greece, 57–58. See also godparents; kinship
Food: staple, of Mayans, 83; of Greeks,
99; classification of, into hot and
cold, 41; sharing of, 82, 110; production of, 134. See also agriculture; diet;
farming
Friendship, sign of, 69

Girls: resentment towards, in rural
Greece, 96; behavior of, and concern
of family's honor, 101
Godparents: 57–58, 70, 73, 82;
responsibilities of, 39. See also fictive
kin
Gossip: 89, 113; exchange of, 83; source
of, 99, 100; abortion as a source of,
114; as a social control, 98; regarding
a widow, 98

Grand parents, attitudes of, toward
small family size, 113
Gypsy, 71
Greek: political party, 57; surnames, 52;
village, description of, 49–53; social
organization, 57

Healers: traditional, Mayans, 41;
h-men, 40, 42, 45, 108; midwives, 84,
43, 63, 114, 117, curandero, 43, 44, 45;
in rural Greece, 59, 61–63. See also
women
Health: beliefs of, in Latin America, 41;
among Mayans, 41–42, 106; in rural
Greece, 59–65; problems of, causes of,
108; concerns of, and menopause,
130; services of, in Mayan villages, 44;
and utilization of, 45, 108; of older
people in rural Greece, 61; practitioners
of, 59. See also, healers
Herbs: medicinal use of, 59, 63, 128,
131; for menstrual pain, 106, 107, 131;
knowledge of, among Mayan women,
123; oregano, 106, 128; rue, 62
Hetzmek: 38, 42; description of, 73.
See also sex role
H-men, 40, 42, 45, 108; as a leader of
Mayan rituals, 42. See also healers
Hormone: reproductive, 132; production of, 131, 133, 137; at menopause,
13; and intake of fat, 134; and body
weight, 134; and genetic factors, 134;
and physical activity, 134; and lactation, 137; changes of, and life cycle,
1, 104; therapy of, 126. See also
estrogen; prolactine
Hot flashes: 13, 15, 20, 116, 122; definition of, 12, 21; and estrogen decline,
123; frequency of, 120; Greek
women's description of, 125; and
management and perception of, 131;
absence of, 119, 123, 130. See also
symptoms
Household: composition of, Mayan,
37–38; Greek, 51–53

Housing: in rural Greece, 51–52, urban Greece, 56; Mayan village, 29–30

Human Relations Area File, 21, 23

Hunters-gatherers, see !Kung

Hygiene: in rural Greece, 64–65; Mayans, 47

Humoral pathology, 41

Illness: symptoms of, 41; afalos, 62; anemia, 122, 123, 135; dengue, 48; evil eye, 45, 61–62; jaundice, 62; pasmo, 105, 106; pellagra, 134; tipte, 46

Infant, mortalility of, 110–111

Infertility: 43; treatment of, by Mayan midwives, 117; lactational, 137. See also amenorrhea

Irritability, 131. See also symptoms

Jerusalem, 69

!Kung: fertility patterns, of, 136

Kinship: 37–39, 57–58. See also fictive kin

Lactation: 132; length of, among Mayan women, 88, 111; among Greek women, 114; effect of, on ovarian function, 137; and amenorrhea, 111, 132; and calcium depletion, 138; and spacing of pregnancy, 111

Land: communal, 135; ownership of, 55; in Mexico, 33; in Yucatan, 134; among Mayans, 33–34; in Greece, 54; and taxes, 57. See also ejido

Life cycle: crisis of, 19–21; events of, 15, 23; medical intervention of, 16; feminist view of, 19; of traditional Greek women, 3. See also reproduction

Maize: planting of, 33, 34; products of, 82. See also agriculture; diet; farming

Malnutrition: protein, 134, 135; and onset of menarche, 133; and post-partum amenorrhea, 133; among Mayans, 117

Marriage: in Greek culture, 54; in Mayan, 84; and kinship, 37, 38; age at, Mayan, 38, 111; Greek, 112. See also dowry; kinship

Maya, geographical area of, 4, 27

Mayan: physical characteristics of, 30; surnames of, 30; village, 27–33, social organization, 36

Men, status of, 89

Menopause: myths of, 16; definition of, 11; biomedical, 2, 12; feminist critique of, 16–19; as deficiency disease, 2, 17–18; as neurosis, 17; hormonal changes at, 11; and osteoporosis, 1, 116, 13–14, 24–25; psychology of, 12–15; cross-cultural findings in, 2–3, 5, 20–25; factors affecting, 2; attitudes toward, American women, 20; in non-Western Societies, 20–22; rural Greek women, 124, 130; Mayan women, 118, 121, 122, 123; perception of, Mayan, 119, 138; age for onset of, Mayan, 119; Greek, 124; experience of, Greek, 123–126; Mayan, 118–123; comparison of, Greek and Mayan, 129; opinions of physicians on, regarding Mayan women, 115–117, 120; Greek women, 126; opinions of traditional Mayan healers on, 117; premature, 131; and fear of emotional problems, 125. See also symptoms; women

Menarche: defined, 103; appearances of secondary sex characteristics at, 103; age for onset of, 104; factors affecting onset of, 104; average age at onset of, Mayan, 104; Greek, 106. See also menses; menstrual cycle, menstruation

Menses, irregular, 117, frequency of, 116. See menstruation

Menstrual blood: 119; retention of, as causes of health problems, 105, 126; perception of, Mayan, 105; Greek, 107

Menstrual cramps, 43; and home remedies, 106. See also pasmo

Menstrual cycle: disorder of 43; treatment of, irregularities of, 128; and diet, 133; and fertility patterns, 136–37

Menstruation: 3, 5; stages of, 7; myths of, 16; cessation of, 130; attitudes toward, Mayan women, 106, 121; Greek women, 107; perception of, Mayan 104; Greek 106–107; experience of, Mayan, 104; Greek, 107; as a sign of good health, 107, 126. See also menses; menstrual blood; taboos

Mestizo: 34, 69, 70; definition of, in Yucatan, 31; in Mexico, 31; outfit of, description of, 32; economic conditions of, 34

Mexico: constitution of, 33; political party of, 36, 37; ministry of health of, 44; government of, 109

Midwife: roles of, 43, 63, 114, 117. See also healers; women

Migration: history of, Greeks, 55; Mayan, 35; reasons for, 35–36, 55

Milpa, system, 33, 87. See agriculture; farming

Modesty, sense of, in Greek tradition, 98; and family honor, 96. See also women

Mongolian spot, 30

Mother: 108; authority of, over sons, 86; status of, 98; relationship with son, 80–81, 97

Mother-in-law: 108; status of, 88, 129

Myths: about menopause, 22–23; about life cycle events, 16

National Institute of Health, 23

National Women's Health Organization Movement, 16–17, 18

Network, establishing, in Greek and Mayan community, 67–70

Nutrition: deficiency of, 134, 135; and reproduction, 133. See also diet; malnutrition

Occupations: of Mayans, 33: rural Greeks, 53–54. See also agriculture; farming

Older women: status of, in extended family, 97; as healers, 62; roles of, 129. See also healers; women

Oregano, use of, 106, 128. See also herbs

Osteoporosis: 116; etiology of, 13–14, 24–25; prevention of, 136; and fertility pattern, 138; and physical activity, 136, 139; and hot flashes, 131; and menopause, 1; and calcium, 13; in non-Western societies, 24–25

Ovary, aging of, 1, 12, 13. See also estrogen; hormone; menopause

Pain, endurance of, 60

Parasites, prevalence of, 135

Pasmo: definition of, 105; causes of, 105, 106. See also menstruation

Pellagra, 134

Pinole, defined, 82. See also food; maize

Political organization: 36–37; and women's roles in, 84

Pozole, defined, 81, 82. See also food; maize

Pregnancy: 3, 132; symptoms of, 111, 114, 123, fear of, 121, 129; complications of, 116; effects of, on ovarian function, 137; number of, Mayan, 111; Greek, 112; attitudes toward, 111; and stress, 88, 114, 124; and appropriate age, in Greek culture, 114; management of, 112

Priest, 63. See also healers; religion

Progestrone, level of, during lactation, 137. See also hormone

Prolactin: effect of, 138; on ovarian steroid production, 137; levels of, in lactating women, 137. See also hormone

Protein: 133; animal, consumption of, 135; deficiency of, 82, 135. See also diet; malnutrition

Puberty, 11, 17; hormonal changes at, 104. See also menarche

Rebellion, Mayan, see Cast war

Religion: Catholic, 38; evangelical, 40, 108; Mayan, 39–40; Greek Orthodox, 58. See also rituals

Reproduction: female, medicalization of, 17; cultural meanings attached to, 20; and nutrition, 133; histories of, Greek and Mayan women, 128–131. See also fertility

Ritual: religious, 58, 109; of Roman Catholic, 39, 69; Mayan, 39; for deceased relatives, 110; of Mayan and Catholic traditions, 40; curative, 42, 46; preventive, 46

Roles: changes of, at menopause, 2, 3, 120, 131; in Western cultures, 15; loss of, 18; constrains of, and life cycle, 20. See also taboos; women

Rue, use of, 62. See also herbs

Sexism, in Western culture, 16, 17, 23

Sex role: Mayan ceremonies of, 42, 73; learning of, 73–80, 96, 100. See also hetzmek

Sexual activity and menopause, 121

Shame, sense of, as qualities in Greek women, 89, 98, 124. See also girls; women

Slash-and-burn, see agriculture; farming

Sons, preference of, 96, 97

Sorcery, 41, 45, 63; and illness, 108

Spirit, of the deceased, 110

Status: economic, and menopausal symptoms, 15–16; and attitudes toward menopause, 19; loss of, at menopause, 18; gain of, at middle age, 3, 80; and aging, 130; and menopausal age, 22, 127; of never married Mayan women, 84, Greek women, 97, 98. See also menopause; women

Stenaxoria, see stress; worry

Sterility: female, a ground for divorce, 108; Mayan etiology of, 108; and old age, 109; adolescent, 133. See also infertility

Stress: causes of, among Mayan women, 85; widows, 86; Greek women, 101, 102; of pregnancy and childbirth, 123; work load, 88. See also alcoholism; worry

Symptoms: of menopause, physiological, 2, 12; hot flashes, 12, 116, 120; irregular menses, hemorrhage, 117, 122; dizzy spells, 122, 124, headache, 122, 124; bochorno, 119; insomnia, 124; irritability, 124, 131, melancholia, 124, 131; psychological, 12, 14; susceptibility to, 16; comparison of, 131; absence of, 21, 23, 117, 123, 126, 127; of menstruation, 105; of pregnancy, nausea, vomiting, fatigue, backaches, 111, 114; of fever, 120. See also illness

Taboos: associated with childbearing, 107, 127, 128; with menstrual blood, 3, 104, 105, 128; sexual, Greek, 113; of food and drinks during menstruation, 105, 106, 107; activities during menstruation, 106; removal of, at menopause, 3, 120, 131

Time, concept of, in Mayan culture, 4

Tipte, defined, 46. See also illness

Tortillas, consumption of, 81, 135. See also food; maize

Urbanization, impact of, in rural Greece, 97

Urban lifestyle, attitudes of older Greeks toward, 56

Vasomotor, changes of, 13. See also
hot flashes

Vegetables: chaya, 82; planting of, 53.
See also agriculture; diet; farming

Vitamins, deficiency of, among
Mayans, 132. See also diet;
malnutrition

Wheat, planting of, 99. See also
agriculture; diet; farming

Widow: in Greek culture, 53; status of,
98. See also women

Women: Greek, 3, 4; characteristics of,
8–9, 101, activities of, 98-100; 98;
status of, 89; unmarried, 98;
postmenopausal, 97, 98; roles of, 97;
sexual modesty of, 89; moral codes of,
71; Mayan; 4, 68, activities of, 73,
81-84, 87-88; characteristics of, 7-8,
85; moral codes of, 80; status of, 80;
roles of never married, 84; as healers,
43, 59, 61-63, 84, 114, 117; divorced,
85; political participation of, 84

World War II, impact of, on fertility in
Greece, 112

Worry, causes of, 87-88, 108, 109. See
also stress

Youth, idealization of, 22, 23